Roads Less Traveled
IN NORTH-CENTRAL OREGON

A Guide to Back Roads and Special Places

Third Edition

[signature]

Steve Arndt

About the Roads Less Traveled Series:

"The series will stitch together the state's history and habitat for anyone who pays as much attention to what they're driving through as where they're going." — **Bill Monroe, *The Oregonian***

www.roadslesstraveledoregon.com

Also by Steve Arndt:

Roads Less Traveled in Northeast Oregon
Roads Less Traveled in Northwest Oregon I
Roads Less Traveled in Northwest Oregon II
Roads Less Traveled in Southeast Oregon
Roads Less Traveled in South-Central Oregon
Roads Less Traveled in Southwest Oregon
The Best of Roads Less Traveled Across Oregon
Oregon Ghost Towns A to Z - Volume 1
Oregon Ghost Towns A to Z - Volume 2
Oregon Ghost Towns A to Z - Volume 3

Roads Less Traveled in North–Central Oregon, Third Edition
A Guide to Back Roads and Special Places

Steve Arndt

Photographs by
Diane Arndt of Woodburn, Oregon

Maps by
Justin Eslinger, Box Lunch Design

Printed in the United States of America

ISBN: 978-0-9844294-6-2

Front Cover:
   A road less traveled between Simnasho and Warm Springs
   (Photograph by Diane Arndt)

Back Cover (from top to bottom)
   Mt. Hood as seen between Dufur and Friend
   Church in Simnasho
   Barn in Rice
   Woolery House in Ione
   Grain Elevator near Boyd
   (Photographs by Diane Arndt)

Designed by

Justin Eslinger | Box Lunch Design
boxlunchdesign@gmail.com

Dedicated to my beloved children

Amanda, Rob and Steve

Young adults journeying on life's roads less traveled and the passengers on many trips mentioned in this series of books.

I shall be telling this with a sigh
Somewhere ages and ages hence:
Two roads diverged in a wood, and I—
I took the one less traveled by,
And that has made all the difference.

—Robert Frost (1874-1963)
from his poem, "The Road Not Taken"

Acknowledgements

Special Thanks to:

- **Debra Holbrook of Shaniko**
  owner and operator of the Shaniko Sage Saloon and Trading Post Museum and gift shop, for providing much needed information about Shaniko and its history

- **James Halliday of Warm Springs**
  for taking time to visit with us about the history of Warm Springs

- **The Warm Springs Museum**
  for providing critical tribal and historic information regarding the Warm Springs Reservation and people

- **Darla Seale, owner of Country Flowers in Condon**
  for sharing information about her community

- **Dufur Museum**
  for photo opportunities and archival history about Dufur

- **Kraemer's Market in Dufur**
  for their excellent sausage

- **Wasco Library**
  for providing information about Wasco, city and county

- **William and Linda Benedict**
  who welcomed us into their beautiful Wasco home

- **Glenn Green, Alfalfa storeowner**
  who drove us to the Pioneer Grave site

- **Brightwood Store**
  who opened up their archives of local and historical information

- **Hood River Chamber of Commerce and Visitors Center**

- **The Dalles Visitors Center**

- **Dave and Jane (DePriest) Wilson of Georgia**
  who we met in Friend and for giving us information about this small community

- **Tom Robinson, manger of the Breitenbush Hot Springs**
  for giving us a guided tour of the beautiful renewal center

- **Bend Visitors Center**

- **Redmond Visitors Center**

- **Culver Visitors Center**

- **Metolius City Hall**
  for providing information about the community

- **Bob Parker, friend and Rufus orchard owner**

- **Moro County Museum**

- **Madras Visitors Center**

- **Bill and Nancy Wilson of Wilson Ranch Retreat Bed and Breakfast in Fossil**

- **Tom Mashos of Big Timber Family Restaurant in Fossil**

- **Misty Stromme, Warner Pacific College**
  for proofreading and editing

- **Diane Arndt**
  for proofreading and editing

- **Charity D. Darnall**
  for editing and proofing the copy

And sincere apologies to anyone we did not mention by name that provided assistance in any way to make this travel book happen. We truly thank you.

Contents

North-Central Oregon

OREGON

Introduction

The first trip in this book, Hood River to Brightwood, was the seed that grew into the Roads Less Traveled series. In August of 2001, as my wife and I have done so frequently, we investigated, planned and then followed a new and lesser-traveled route. This trip took us around the north side of Mt. Hood, a road that gently meanders from Dee to Zig Zag through one of the most recent of Mt. Hood's volcanic lava eruptions.

For what ever reason, I did some extra research on this route, discovering that Captain Albert Walker, who would go on to fight in the Civil War, tried to develop an alternative northern crossing to Sam Barlow's southern route around the mountain. Walker was intent on finding and building an easier route for pioneers, saving them from the dreaded descent down Laurel Hill. The route was scheduled to follow an ancient Native American trade route, which allowed Native Americans from the valley to trade with Indians from the North, as well as fish for salmon in the waters of the Columbia. The Celilo Falls area, near the Dalles, was the major meeting place for annual trading and fishing.

Driving this route, whose course has changed little since the 1850s, will give the traveler an idea of how easy this grade would have been. However, it was not to be as Captain Walker was met with resistance at every turn, from having to pay over-inflated prices for needed materials, being denied access to workers and not being able to receive much needed credit for supplies and construction costs. Walker was stonewalled so frequently, he eventually abandoned his project, going bankrupt in the process.

Introduction

Further research showed that Walker's route was designed to take pioneers near and through the Bull Run Watershed, the source of Portland's drinking water. Even though this travel friendly route around the mountain would have

saved thousands of hours and many lives, Portland's movers and shakers at the time were the ones responsible for sabotaging Walkers work. Their motive: not wanting their water source contaminated by settlers who would destroy the purity of the water with their wagons, families and livestock. Bankrupt, Walker left the Oregon Territory in the latter 1850s to join the US Army, rising to the rank of Captain during the Civil War, never returning west to the place that he dearly loved.

Much of the content of this book deals with the Oregon Trail. The second trip, Detroit to Warm Springs, takes the traveler near the site of Fort Deposit, a fort designed to hold wagon trail blazing materials during the snowy winter of 1845. Materials were cached at this location as the weather prohibited further travel. A member of the Barlow work crew stayed behind to watch the materials that were housed here until the spring melt. Many and long sections of the Oregon Trail can be accessed and easily walked, with every chapter having a connection to our pioneer heritage.

With the driving of the Golden Spike in 1869, many people, who previously walked the Oregon Trail behind their wagons, could now ride the rails to the newly created state of Oregon. Months of travel time was eliminated, hardships and the toil of the journey eased, though the cost increased. Many easterners were forced to continue the westward passage in wagons, albeit in lesser numbers,

Introduction

as settlers could not afford the costs charged by the railroad. As late as the early 1900s, just prior to the advent of the automobile, the last few people made the trek west to Oregon. State lines, private ownership of land, and fences kept more people from making the sojourn westward. Many little communities and towns sprung up along the wagon routes, often formed by settlers that could go no farther. As towns appeared so did schools and churches, which were on the path of wagons proceeding west. Imagine being a student in one of these old schools, playing at recess in late September and watching a wagon train pass, or leaving church services in early October and seeing newcomers to the state arriving in prairie schooners.

Take this book with you as you take the Roads Less Traveled in North Central Oregon, but also take your imaginations and sensitivities, reflecting on the struggle our forefathers endured to settle this territory and state. Walk reverently along the remnants of the Oregon Trail, envisioning a grave every 10 yards and visualizing the trail as pioneers did 150 years ago. In many places, little has changed since Barlow established his pioneer road. Are you up to the task? Can you hear conversations of families, the voices of wagon masters or feel the grief caused by the loss of a loved one en route to a foreign place? Are you able to hear the same wind blow, feel the same rainfall, and sense the same seasons change, just as they did scores of years past? Are you able to feel, intuitively, the joy, the agony, and the sacrifices made by these hardy folk? If so, this book is for you.

Steve Arndt

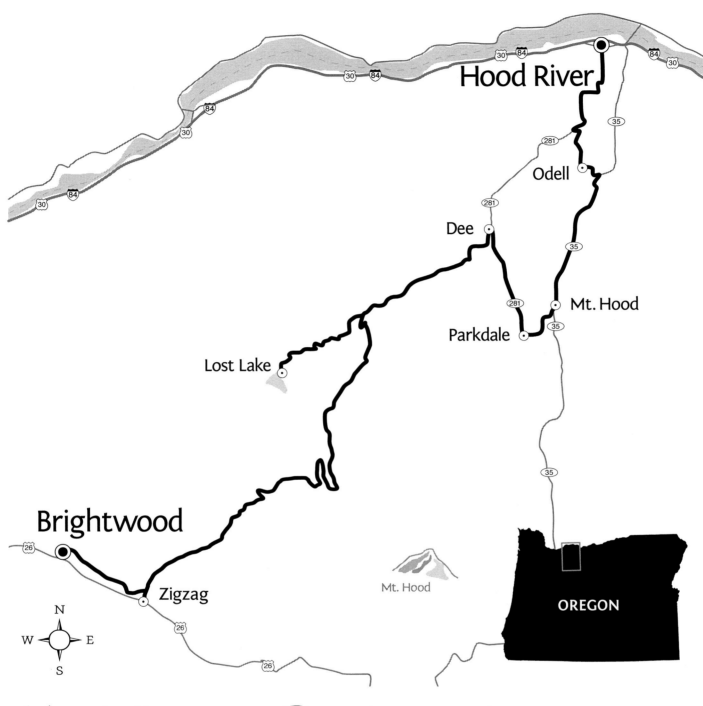

Hood River to Brightwood

1

Captain Walker's Answer to Sam Barlow's Trail

Hood River to Brightwood (72 miles)

This trip explores the north side of Mount Hood, Oregon's most famous peak and one of the most frequently scaled mountains in the United States. Known to Native Americans as Wy'east, Mount Hood rises 11,235 feet, making it the highest point in the state. It was formed by volcanic activity some 500,000 years ago, with minor eruptions as recently as 1907. Had explorers Lewis and Clark come one year earlier, they might have witnessed the mountain venting steam and spewing ash in the 1804 eruption. Evidence of earlier eruptions, including lava flows less than 300 years old, are visible along this route that follows a millennia-old Indian trade and migration trail, when, fall and spring, thousands of Native Americans left the forests and meadows of the Willamette Valley to trade and fish at Celilo Falls.

This is the same route that Captain Albert Walker, intent on saving emigrants from the dreaded descent of Laurel Hill, tried to develop in the 1850s as an alternative to Sam Barlow's southern route around the mountain. Driving today along this route, whose course has changed little since the 1850s; travelers will get an idea of how easy the grade and the trip would have been. But it was not to be. Walker's route would have taken pioneers through the Bull Run Watershed, the source of Portland's drinking water. Even though it may have saved thousands of hours and many lives, Portland's movers and shakers at the time sabotaged Walker's work. Their motive: protecting their water source from contamination by settlers and their livestock.

As a result, Walker met resistance at every turn, from paying inflated prices for materials, to being denied workers as well as credit for supplies and construction costs. In fact, Walker was stonewalled so frequently that he eventually abandoned his project, going bankrupt in the process. He left Oregon in the late 1850s to join the US Army, rising to the rank of Captain during the Civil War, never returning to the place he dearly loved.

Lolo Pass road

From Mount Hood, Walker's route ambles through peach, cherry and apple orchards on the way to the small community of Brightwood, near Sandy. Along the way, it passes through the ghost-like remains of the Dee Lumber Mill, over several pristine streams, through recent lava flows, and on to Lost Lake, where eagles soar across the sky. In addition, seasonal changes make this seldom-seen north side of Mount Hood beautiful year-around, though a well maintained, hard-packed gravel road that meanders gently for about five miles of the trip is often closed following the first snow.

Hood River

Elevation: 110 feet

Location:
45.42.581 N • 121.30.685 W

Services:
gas, food, lodging, B&B

Hood River was named to honor Lord Samuel Hood, expedition sponsor of Captain Robert Gray's voyages. The name is given to the community and the river, which was first called Dog River, as famished pioneers consumed canine flesh to survive. The post office opened in 1858; the town was platted in 1881 and incorporated in 1895. Hood River began to flourish in the 1880s once the railroad lines reached town. The 1910 spur to Parkdale, which can be taken today, allowed for timber to be cut and hauled into town for milling. Once the trees were removed, pioneer families discovered that fruit trees would flourish, making the Hood River Valley famous for apples, peaches, cherries and pears. Hood River is the county seat and its center of commerce.

Hood River Hotel

Points of Interest

- **Mt. Hood Hotel** *(1st and Oak)*
Constructed of brick in 1912, it replaced the wooden hotel that was built in 1881. It is known today as the Hood River Hotel.

- **Railroad Depot**
(between 1st and 2nd and Cascade)
This 1906 depot replaced the 1882 original. It is now home to the Mt. Hood Railway Co., which offers excursions to Parkdale.

- **City Hall** *(2nd and State)*
Built in 1921, it originally housed the jail and the fire department.

- **Old Hotel Waucoma**
(2nd and Cascade)
Erected in 1904, the hotel receives its name from the Native American word *waucoma*, which means cottonwood, and was the name given to the area by the earliest pioneers to arrive here.

- **E.L. Smith Building**
(3rd and Oak)
Original home of the 1904 First National Bank.

- **International Museum of Carousel Art** *(304 Oak St)*
Over 100 carousel art figures are displayed in this not for profit museum.

- **IOOF Hall** *(4th and Oak)*
This downtown building is the town's last remaining wooden business structure. The downstairs was once the Paris Department Store while the IOOF met upstairs.

- **Columbia Art Gallery**
(101 4th St)
Local and regional artisans display their works.

- **Union Building** *(extends between 3rd and 4th on Columbia)*
Opened in 1905, this is the oldest fruit packing facility in the valley.

- **Hood River County Library**
(State street, between 4th and 6th)
Funded by the Carnegie Foundation, the library has served the county since 1913.

- **Hood River Historical Museum** *(300 E. Port Marina Dr)*
Holds a variety of pioneer and Native American artifacts.

- **Hood River Visitors Center**
(405 Portway Drive)
Many displays, numerous brochures and a knowledgeable staff.

- **Elliot Park** *(12th Street)*
Picnic area overlooks the town and river. Restrooms, playground, shelter.

- **Columbia Gorge Hotel**
  (4000 Westcliff Drive)
  This famous and elegant hotel opened in 1921. The Inn was recently remodeled with a new addition.

- **Cathedral Ridge Winery**
  (4200 Post Canyon Dr)
  Beautiful views and excellent wines.

Hood River to Odell

Distance:
6.9 miles

Directions:
From 13th and Oak, proceed south on 13th.

Points En Route

(mileage from 13th and Oak)

1.8 miles:
St. Mary's Cemetery, dating to the 1890s, is one of three cemeteries that adjoin at this location.

3.2 miles:
Turn left onto Indian Creek Road.

3.6 miles:
Ken Jernstedt Airport

5.1 miles:
The Apple Valley Country store, in a 100-year old farmhouse, serves and sells old fashioned milkshakes, crafts, jams, jellies, and seasonal produce.

5.2 miles:
Stay left to Odell.

5.7 miles:
Fred Lane Ranch, established in 1905. Note views of Mt. Hood.

6.9 miles:
Odell

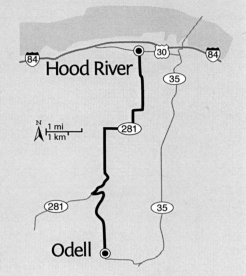

Pine Grove/Odell United Methodist Church

Odell

Elevation: 723 feet

Location:
45.38.109 N • 121.32.807 W

Services:
gas, food, lodging, B&B

The community was named for William Odell, an 1861 settler. The post office opened in 1910 under the name of Newtown, and was changed in 1911, the same year the railroad came through town. Lots of fruit production, including cherries, peaches, pears and apples, keep the community economically sound. Odell is home to the Hood River County Fair.

Points of Interest

- **Odell School**
  (one block west on Summit)
  Built in 1910 as Newtown School, the name changed in 1911 to Odell School.

- **Church of Christ**
  (across from the old school on Summit)
  After nearly 100 years, services are still held here every Sunday.

- **IOOF Hall and Rebekah Lodge** *(intersection of Odell Highway and Summit Road)*
  The old building was the center of community activity.

- **Pine Grove/Odell United Methodist Church** *(corner Eagle Loop Road and Atkinson)*
  Built in 1919.

- **Shelley Cemetery**
  (off Sunday Drive)
  The cemetery dates to 1900 and is 0.7 miles east of town.

- **Naked Winery Tasting Room**
  (102 2nd)
  Their mantra; 'Drink Naked!'

4

old wagon between Odell and Mt. Hood

Mt. Hood

Elevation: 1,555 feet

Location:
45.32.305 N • 121.34.113 W

Services: food

Mt. Hood receives its name from the 11,235-foot mountain that towers above the rural community. The post office opened in the general store in 1902, and closed in 1976.

Points of Interest

- **1902 Store:** *(intersection of Highway 35 and Cooper Spur Road)* A 1935 addition to the store – the right side of the current building – more than tripled its original size. Many old photos of the community line its side, while inside are groceries, antiques, a deli and café.

- **Mt. Hood School** *(across the street from the store)* The first school was established in 1890, with the current 1905 building serving as the community center. There is a historical marker next to the highway in front of the school.

Odell to Mt. Hood

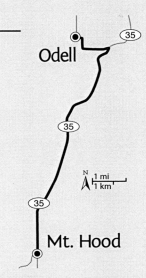

Odell

35

35

35

Mt. Hood

N
1 mi
1 km

Distance:
7.5 miles

Directions:
From the intersection of Eagle Loop Road and Odell Highway, go left, following the signs toward Highway 35.

Points En Route

(mileage from Eagle Loop Road and the Odell Highway)

0.2 miles:
Hood River Lavender Gardens

0.8 miles:
Intersection with state Highway 35. Turn right, traveling south.

3.4 miles:
Viewpoint.

4.0 miles:
An operating lumber mill, one of the few that remain.

4.5 miles:
Middle Valley School, now a private residence, operated from the 1920s until the 1960s.

7.5 miles:
Mt. Hood

Mt. Hood School

Mt. Hood to Parkdale

Distance:
  1.9 miles

Directions:
  From the Mt. Hood Country Store, proceed west toward Parkdale.

Points En Route

(mileage from the Mt. Hood Country Store)

0.8 miles:
  Crossing the East Fork of Hood River.

1.7 miles:
  Turn right to Parkdale.

1.9 miles:
  Parkdale

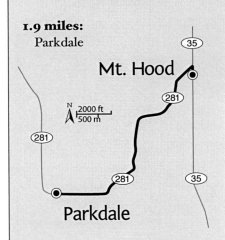

Parkdale

Elevation: 1,663 feet

Location:
45.31.172 N • 121.35.401 W

Services: food, B&B

Parkdale was named for its "park-like" qualities and beautiful setting against the mountain. The post office opened in 1910, the same year the railroad spur from Hood River was completed. Parkdale, which thrives on tourism, is a community with fruit and vegetable production as its main economy.

old Parkdale movie theater

Points of Interest

- **Old Parkdale Movie Theater** *(on Baseline downtown)*
  Now home to the Elliot Glacier Public House, the original theater opened in the 1930s. The old marquis still hangs over the building.

- **Parkdale Mt. Hood National Forest Work Center** *(on Baseline Drive)*
  Built during the Depression, the facility was upgraded in the 1970s.

- **Parkdale Inn** *(4932 Baseline)*
  A bed and breakfast establishment housed in one of Parkdale's oldest homes.

- **Parkdale Community Presbyterian Church** *(Baseline and 4th)*
  The beautiful stained glass windows of this 1911 church are noteworthy.

- **Hutson Museum** *(on Baseline near the railroad tracks)*
  Constructed to look old, the museum tells of Parkdale's early history. It includes an extensive collection of Native American artifacts and a large display of rock specimens.

Parkdale

Points of Interest (continued)

- **Parkdale Railroad Depot Park** *(the end of the Mt. Hood Railway)*
  At the intersection of Baseline and the Dee Highway, Clear Creek Park is the terminus for the railroad, and offers picnicking with a spectacular view of Mt. Hood's north face.

- **Ries-Thompson House** *(in Clear Creek Park)*
  The oldest residence in Parkdale, built in 1900.

- **Parkdale Community Center** *(7300 Clear Creek Road)*
  Across the street from the railroad and park, the center operates out of the old Parkdale School that opened in 1910.

- **Parkdale Grange #500** *(7375 Clear Creek Road)*
  The old, white building stands vacant.

- **Kiyokawa Family Orchards** *(8129 Clear Creek Road)*
  A family operation since 1944, the Kiyokawa's grow over seventy varieties of apples and pears. Watch for special events at their farm.

- **Lava Springs** *(west of town on Baseline Road to Lave Bed Road)*
  One of the area's numerous freshwater springs.

- **Upper Valley Cemetery** *(Allen Road)*
  Opened in 1912.

Ries-Thompson House

Parkdale to Dee

Distance:
5.4 miles

Directions:
From Baseline Road and Clear Creek Road, travel north on the Dee Highway.

Points En Route

(mileage from Baseline and Clear Creek Road)

3.8 miles:
Former community of Trout Creek.

5.0 miles:
Dee water tower and mill.

5.2 miles:
Turn left.

5.4 miles:
Dee

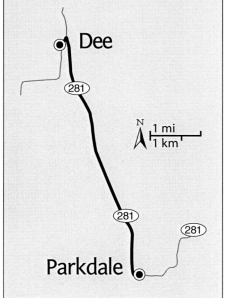

Dee

Elevation: 988 feet

Location:
45.35.368 N • 121.37.674 W

Services: none

Not much remains of Dee, a community that prospered and grew around the Oregon Lumber Company Mill. The mill, which opened in 1906, brought hundreds of workers to the area. Dee, named to honor Judge Thomas Dee, has a few isolated homes near the skeletal walls of the old mill. The post office closed in 1959, coinciding with the mill closure. *Ripley's Believe It Or Not* made mention of Dee in the 1930s, calling it a "back door town" because every front porch faced the railroad tracks rather than the street. All of these homes were removed when the mill shut down.

Points of Interest

- **Hood River** *(near the old mill)*
  The river cuts a path, separating the mill from former homes of workers and the school. Some of the old mill buildings, which stand next to the river, are used for storage and commerce.

- **Punchbowl Road**
  (take Punchbowl Road, going up the hill and to the right)
  The road leads to Punchbowl Falls, 3.2 miles from Dee. A picturesque and easy hike to the falls. Picnic area and primitive restrooms.

abandoned Oregon Lumber Company Mill

Dee to Lost Lake

Distance:
13.6 miles

Directions:
From the bridge, turn left onto Lost Lake Road.

Points En Route

(mileage from the bridge)

0.7 miles:
The old Dee School, now privately owned, opened in 1906 (the same year as the mill) and served children of forest product workers.

1.5 miles:
Dee Fire Department.

2.7 miles:
Old restaurant.

5.8 miles:
Road becomes Forest Road 13.

7.9 miles:
Turn right to Lost Lake. The road, while paved, is winding and narrow. Slower speeds are recommended.

13.6 miles:
Lost Lake

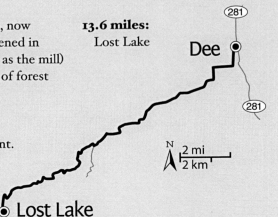

Lost Lake

Elevation: 3,111 feet

Location:
45.29.788 N • 121.49.130 W

Services: food, camping

Lost Lake

Lost Lake is a popular resort destination. The old lodge, destroyed by fire, has been replaced by a modern structure, built to blend into the woodsy surroundings. Two different stories exist about the naming of the lake. The first says that an 1880 hunting party reached the lake after getting lost along the way. The other is a Native American legend about a white deer that came out of the woods, swam to the middle of the lake, and drowned. Those who witnessed the drowning took it as a bad omen and vowed never to camp near the lake's waters. Some years later, a young Indian couple defied tribal wisdom by camping on the lakeshore, and were killed by lightning.

Nowadays, amenities at the lake include fishing, swimming (albeit chilly waters), picnicking, boating, camping, and wildlife viewing. Visitors often spot bald eagles and osprey, and fishermen come for the abundant kokanee salmon as well as brook, rainbow and brown trout. A two-mile hike leads to Lost Lake Butte, which affords a panoramic view of the lake and mountain. Evidence of the 1886 Ghost Ridge Fire can still be seen near Cloud Cap Pass.

Lost Lake General Store

Lost Lake to Zigzag

Distance:
30.0 miles

Directions:
From Lost Lake, backtrack 5.7 miles on Forest Road 13.

Points En Route

(mileage from Lost Lake Store)

5.7 miles:
Forest Road 13 intersects with Forest Road 18. Turn right.

6.5 miles:
Crossing the West Fork of Hood River.

6.7 miles:
Logging clear-cut.

8.8 miles:
Intersection with Vista Ridge Road. Stay right on Forest Road 18.

10.0 miles:
Evidence of the most recent eruption on Mt. Hood. Several eruptions occurred in the early and mid 1800s.

11.7 miles:
Wooden deck bridge.

11.9 miles:
Slow down: the road was washed out and repaired.

12.0 miles:
Fork in road, stay left on pavement.

13.8 miles:
Mazama Trail Marker. Pavement ends, changing to 5.5 miles of well-maintained gravel and hard-packed dirt.

16.0 miles:
Elevation: 3,000 feet.

18.1 miles:
Elevation: 3,342 feet. Look for a sign that says "Lolo Pass, 1 mile." Lolo is Chinook jargon for "backpack" or "carry-on," which described how the Native Americans traveled on this north side of the mountain trail.

19.3 miles:
Lolo Pass Summit, 3,390 feet. Pavement returns.

20.8 miles:
Great views of Mt. Hood.

25.8 miles:
Return to two-lane, striped highway.

28.8 miles:
Intersection with Barlow Road; continue straight toward Zigzag.

29.0 miles:
Crossing the Sandy River.

29.7 miles:
Crossing the Zigzag River.

30.0 miles:
Zigzag

Lost Lake

N
2 mi
2 km

26 Zigzag

eruption flow near Lolo Pass

Zigzag

Elevation: 1,458 feet

Location:
45.20.579 N • 121.56.479 W

Services: gas, food, lodging

Zigzag was a resting place on the Barlow Trail after pioneers completed the Laurel Hill descent. Oregon pioneer Joel Palmer named the community after the zigzagging he did on his way here. The name also applies to the nearby river, canyon, glacier, and mountain. A community dependent upon the forest industry and tourism, Zigzag – which had it's own post office from 1917-1974 but never incorporated – has strong economic ties with the U.S. Forest Service, Oregon State Forestry Services, local lumber mills, and tree planting jobbers. According to the North American Meteor Network, on March 19, 2004, a meteor registering a speed of four and magnitude of minus seven was observed here.

Zigzag Ranger Station

Points of Interest

- **Zigzag Ranger Station**
  (near intersection of Highway 26 and Lolo Pass Road)
  Restrooms and forest information. Forest Service headquarters for the district, which forms the western boundary of the Mt. Hood National Forest.

- **Welches** *(one mile west and south)*
  Named for Samuel Welch, an 1882 resident. The post office has operated in Welches since 1905.

- **Wemme** *(two miles west)*
  Named to honor Henry Wemme, who championed to get state ownership of the Barlow Trail Road. Wemme had its own post office from 1916 to 1977. The Barlow Trail is now part of the Mt. Hood Highway.

Zigzag to Brightwood

Distance:
6.3 miles

Directions:
From Zigzag, return 1.1 miles on Lolo Pass Road to E. Barlow Trail Road.

Points En Route

(mileage from intersection of Highway 26 and Lolo Pass Road)

0.2 miles:
Crossing Zigzag River.

1.1 miles:
Turn left onto E. Barlow Trail Road. This is the actual route of the pioneers as they traveled toward Oregon City.

6.0 miles:
Turn left onto E. Brightwood Bridge Road.

6.3 miles:
Brightwood

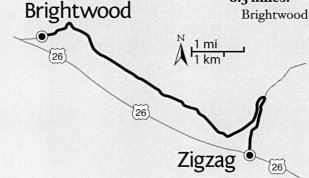

Brightwood

Elevation: 1,141 feet

Location:
45.22.579 N • 122.01.021 W

Services: food, lodging, B&B

Brightwood received is name from the sunlight on the abundant cottonwoods at this location near the river. The first post office opened in 1891 under the name of Salmon, for the nearby Salmon River. The name was changed to Brightwood in 1910. The original Barlow Toll Gate stood near the location of the Brightwood General Store but was moved to its new location 6.0 miles east on Highway 26.

Points of Interest

- **Brightwood Firehouse**
  (next to the store)
  Built in the late 1920s.

- **Brightwood General Store**
  (on main road)
  Constructed in 1910, the store was moved to its present location in 1923 after a devastating flood.

- **Brightwood Tavern**
  (across from the store)
  A local watering hole since 1920.

Brightwood is only 0.7 miles west of Highway 26. To reach the highway, turn right onto East Brightwood Loop Road, which will intersect with Highway 26. Turn right on Highway 26 to reach Sandy. Information on Sandy can be found in *Roads Less Traveled in Northwest Oregon II*.

Brightwood General Store

Brightwood Tavern

Detroit to Warm Springs

Going from Hot Water to Warm Springs

Detroit to Warm Springs (134 miles)

Beginning at the former lumber town of Detroit, now a popular recreation destination, this road twists and turns over the Cascade Range to the pine-dotted eastern side of the state. The paved route – seldom used except by hikers, campers and anglers – begins on Forest Road 46.

The first legs are slow, picturesque meanders to Breitenbush and then to Wamic, a route that follows or crosses parts of the Oregon Trail and affords easy hikes along this pathway of the pioneers. In contrast, Breitenbush is a commune that offers an alternative lifestyle to guests and visitors seeking meditation or relaxation. After crossing the Cascade summit, the road passes several abandoned schoolhouses and churches that are haunting reminders of days when communities flourished here.

The trip ends in Warm Springs, the cultural center of the Confederated Tribes of the Paiute, Wasco, and Warm Springs people. Side trips to Timothy Lake and Government Camp are also possible on this route that crosses several topographical and habitat boundaries.

the road between Breitenbush and Wamic

Detroit

Elevation: 1,585 feet

Location:
44.44.272 N • 122.09.098 W

Services:
gas, food, lodging, B&B, camping

Old Detroit, named by early Michigan settlers after their beloved homeland, was originally located about a half-mile north of its present location before the 1953 construction of the 463-foot high Detroit Dam covered the site with water. The town prospered during the dam's construction and flourished until the harvest of old-growth timber ended. Today, Detroit and its reservoir are a mecca for boaters, hunters, campers, and anglers, while the dam provides flood control and generates over 100 megawatts of electrical power.

Detroit Lake

Points of Interest

- **Detroit School**
  (Patton Road and Santiam Avenue)
  The 1950s school is closed, with current students bussed to Mill City.

- **Community Gym**
  (Patton and Santiam)
  Adjacent to the old school, the gym serves as the community center for the town's tightly knit inhabitants.

- **Detroit Flats Recreation Area**
  (Follow Santiam Avenue toward the lake)
  Picnic tables, restrooms, a boat launch and fishing are available in this lesser known area of town.

- **Detroit Community Church**
  (200 Detroit Avenue)
  The first church in the relocated town opened its doors in 1953.

- **Mongold State Park**
  (1.2 west of Detroit)
  Day use fees, restrooms, changing areas, swim beach and boat ramp.

- **Detroit Ranger Station**
  (across from the State Park on Highway 22, 3.0 miles west of town)
  A newly constructed facility, with much information about the area.

- **Detroit Lake State Park**
  (on the lake side of Highway 22, across from the Ranger Station)
  133 tent sites, 106 full hook-up sites and 72 electrical sites are available for camping enjoyment. Reservations are recommended. Call 1-800-452-5687.

Community Gym

original homestead cabin

Breitenbush

Elevation: 2,320 feet

Location:
44.46.743 N • 121.58.412 W

Services: food, lodging

NOTE: The Breitenbush Hot Springs area is a communal sanctuary for meditation, reflection and yoga. Clothing is optional in the numerous tiled and rock-lined natural spring hot tubs.

Named for an 1840s explorer in the area, the Breitenbush post office opened in 1928 but moved to Detroit in 1953 when construction on the dam was completed. The springs, part of the most active geothermal areas in the state, were first homesteaded in 1904, with communal living taking root in the early 1980s. Today the commune owns and operates 154 acres that surround numerous hot springs as well as the original homestead cabin. Three meadow pools, four tiled tubs, and a sauna are open twenty-four hours a day. In the 1930s, more than fifty hot tubs and pools were available for public use. The main lodge, erected more than seventy-five years ago, houses a vegetarian dining room, library, event space, and guest rooms. Hiking trails lead through old-growth timber, past river cascades, and to magnificent mountain vistas. Lodging costs include all meals. Day use is available for a small fee.

Points of Interest

- **Hot Tub Areas** *(follow pathways)* Tiled and rock-lined tubs range in temperature according to personal comfort.

Detroit to Breitenbush

Distance:
10.4 miles

Directions:
At the intersection of Highway 22 and National Forest Road 46, turn left, traveling northeast, following the Breitenbush River.

NOTE: The next gasoline station is in Maupin, 90 miles from Detroit.

Points En Route

(mileage from the intersection of Highway 22 and Forest Road 46)

0.8 miles:
Park and wayside.

4.4 miles:
Turn-off toward Elk Lake.

4.5 miles:
Humbug Campground. Primitive facilities.

6.3 miles:
Fox Creek group campground.

9.0 miles:
Cleator Bend campground.

9.1 miles:
Turn right onto Forest Road 4693. Pavement ends but gravel road is well maintained.

9.2 miles:
Turn left onto Forest Road 2231.

10.4 miles:
Breitenbush

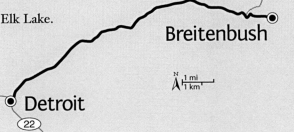

Breitenbush

Points of Interest (continued)

- **Lodge** (*center of the community*)
  The center of activity.

- **Old Homestead** (*behind the lodge*)
  The commune plans to restore the cabin.

- **Hiking Trails** (*miles of trails*)
  Paths lead to beautiful views, and past old growth timber and geothermal pools.

Clackamas Lake Ranger Station

Breitenbush to Wamic

Distance:
77.1 miles

Directions:
From the parking lot, backtrack to Forest Road 46. The next seventy-seven mile route offers limited tourist accommodations and is arguably one of the most scenic and minimally inhabited stretches of state-maintained road in Oregon.

Points En Route

(mileage from the parking lot)

1.2 miles:
Turn right onto Forest Road 4693. Pavement returns.

1.4 miles:
Turn right on Forest Road 46.

1.7 miles:
Breitenbush Campground. Primitive facilities.

8.9 miles:
Entering Mt. Hood National Forest

9.0 miles:
Cascade Mountains forest road summit.

15.2 miles:
Recent lava eruption, 450 years ago.

15.5 miles:
Olallie Lake turn-off.

16.6 mils:
Crossing Clackamas River.

22.3 miles:
Turn right onto Forest Road 42. The single-lane road is paved with ample pullouts.

23.3 miles:
Wooden bridge.

26.6 miles:
Intersection with Forest Roads 42 and 4220. Stay left on Forest Road 42.

30.1 miles:
At the "Y," go left on Forest Road 42 toward Timothy Lake and Highway 26.

30.9 miles:
The single-lane road returns to two lanes.

Wamic

Breitenbush

meadow along the road to Wamic

Old Barlow Road

35.7 miles:
Turn-off to Summit Lake.

40.2 miles:
Clackamas Lake Campground turn-off.

40.5 miles:
Clackamas Lake Historic Ranger Station. The first building, one of eleven, was constructed in 1900. There are nineteen campsites on the 2400-acre site, with picnic grounds, non-motorized boating and horse trails.

40.6 miles:
Clackamas Meadows. The juncture of Oak Grove Creek and the Clackamas River. Look for an old cabin near the waters' edge.

40.7 miles:
Intersection. Stay right, traveling toward Little Crater Lake and Highway 26. For a side trip, Timothy Lake is only two miles to the left.

40.8 miles:
Joe Graham Horse Camp. Primitive restrooms.

42.1 miles:
Entrance to the Warm Springs Indian Reservation.

44.3 miles:
Junction with Highway 58. Stay right, continuing on Forest Road 42.

48.7 miles:
Skyline Sno-Park. Primitive restrooms.

49.1 miles:
Turn right and drive east toward Maupin and Madras.

50.8 miles:
Turn left onto Forest Road 43, traveling toward White River and Wamic. The road is paved but not striped.

56.2 miles:
Road crosses the old Barlow Trail at the site of Fort Deposit, a temporary shelter designed as a cache for supplies during the winter of 1845-46, when snow prevented further travel. A member of the trail's crew stayed behind to watch the fort, its tools and supplies, until

spring. Sections of the Barlow Trail, located on either side of the paved road, are accessible by foot.

56.8 miles:
Intersection with Forest Road 48. Turn right and drive toward Rock Creek Reservoir and Wamic.

65.0 miles:
Note the change from Douglas fir to pine trees, with views of treeless, barren hills in distance.

71.5 miles:
Rock Creek Campround.

73.0 miles:
Leaving Mt. Hood National Forest. The landscape changes abruptly to sagebrush and rabbit brush.

74.2 miles:
The road at this location follows the old Barlow Trail.

74.3 miles:
Mary's Pond.

77.1 miles:
Wamic

Wamic

Elevation: 1,651 feet

Location:
45.13.690 N • 121.16.182 W

Services:
gas, food

Wamic is a misspelling of "Womack," a family of three brothers who settled in the area in the 1870s. The post office opened in 1884 and closed in 1958. Once an important stop on the Barlow Road, Wamic today is an agricultural and timber center, with many cattle ranches surrounding the small community.

windmil, blacksmith and "Rural Station"

Points of Interest

- **Barlow Gate Grange #157**
  (56960 Wamic Market Road)
  Established in 1884 near the site of one of Barlow's Tollgates.

- **Smock Prairie School**
  (Wamic Market Road)
  The old school was used from 1906 to 1956, and moved to this location in 1995. Smock Prairie, which had its own post office for ten years beginning in 1899, was located seven miles southwest, and was named for a pioneer farmer who froze to death near the site of the school. As a fundraiser in the summer, visitors can ring the old school bell for $1.00.

- **Wamic Jail** *(next to Wamic Auto Park on Wamic Market Road)*
  Preserved and moved to this location.

- **Old Houses**
  (Campbell Street and Pioneer Street)
  Several of the older homes in Wamic are situated near this intersection.

- **Old Tree** *(in the yard of the home at 57014 Campbell Street)*
  Pioneers, following the Barlow Trail, camped under this tree en route to Oregon City. The current resident is a descendant of Jesse Applegate.

- **Campbell House**
  (57062 Campbell Street)
  This 1899 home has been restored to look as it did when first constructed.

- **Barlow Trail Site and Tollbooth Location**
  (entrance to Emigrant Street)
  A marker tells of the location of one of Barlow's toll gates. The toll in 1846 was five dollars, a large sum of money at the time.

- **Pratt Cemetery**
  (Emigrant Street)
  Dates to 1868. Note the log structure near the cemetery.

- **Pratt House**
  (80228 Emigrant Street)
  Built in 1878, it is the oldest home in Wamic.

Smock Prairie School

Wamic to Pine Grove

Distance:
15.6 miles

Directions:
From the Wamic General Store, travel southwest by backtracking on the Wamic Market Road to Smock Road. This scenic route contains 6.7 miles of poorly maintained gravel and exposed basalt rock road. For an alternative paved route, drive east on Wamic Market Road to Tygh Valley, and there follow Highway 216 to Wapinitia and Pine Grove. Total distance of the alternative route is 25.0 miles.

Points En Route

(mileage from the Wamic Store)

0.5 miles:
Turn left onto Smock Road.

1.3 miles:
Pioneer homestead.

1.5 miles:
Intersection of Smock Road and Driver Road. Stay left on Smock.

1.9 miles:
Lone Pine Cemetery, dates to 1877.

2.1 miles:
Intersection of Woodcock Road and Smock Road. Stay left on Smock.

4.9 miles:
Gate Creek.

7.4 miles:
Intersection with White River Road. Turn left. At this point the pavement ends and the road becomes rugged but is navigable and scenic. Drive slowly to see how the river has carved the canyon from ancient basalt flows. Exercise extreme caution during inclement weather. The road is not maintained in the winter.

8.3 miles:
Earthen Dam on White Creek.

9.5 miles:
The road winds down and then back up the White River Canyon. The next 2.2 miles is the most difficult part of the route.

9.7 miles:
Crossing the White River at the bottom of the canyon. The White River is appropriately named due to its milky color.

11.7 miles:
Intersection with Victor Road. Turn right toward Pine Grove. The road is graveled but well-maintained.

13.2 miles:
Horse Ranch, a hundred-year-old farm.

14.1 miles:
Intersection with Highway 216, where pavement resumes. Turn right and drive west toward Government Camp.

15.6 miles:
Pine Grove

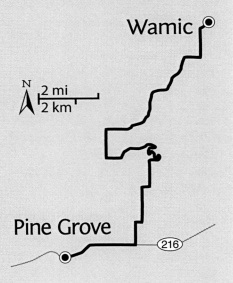

historic tree in Wamic

Pine Grove

Elevation: 1,669 feet

Location:
45.06.860 N • 121.21.221 W

Services:
gas, food, RV Park

Named for the abundance of nearby pine trees, Pine Grove is a 'string town' that stretches along one mile of Highway 216. Once home to many lumber mills, of which only one remains, Pine Grove is a recreational stop for rafters, hunters and anglers. Tourism, farming, and cattle ranching provide a base for the local economy. Lumbermax, a corporation that manufactures redwood, cedar and Trex decking, is located here.

Pine Grove School

Points of Interest

- **Pine Grove Trailer Corral**
  (on the highway)
  Full hook-ups are available for both long and short term camping.

- **Pine Grove Mercantile**
  (on the highway)
  Constsructed and operated in the days when many mills were in full production.

- **Pine Grove School**
  (on the highway)
  Opened in 1911 and closed when the mills began their decline. It is still used as the community center.

- **Juniper Market**
  (west end of the string)
  A convenience market for locals and travelers. Located at the west end of town on the highway.

Pine Grove to Wapinitia

Distance:
7.1 miles

Directions:
From Juniper Market, located at the west end of Pine Grove, backtrack on Highway 216 and head east toward Maupin.

Points En Route

(mileage from the Juniper Store)

1.5 miles:
Intersection with Endersby Road. Continue east on Highway 26.

3.1 miles:
Intersection with Victor Road. A 1.4 mile side trip north on Victor Road leads to Oak Grove and the old Oak Grove School, which today is a residence.

6.1 miles:
Turn right onto Reservation Road, heading toward Wapinitia.

7.1 miles:
Wapinitia

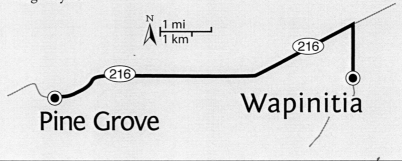

Wapinitia

Elevation: 2,053 feet

Location:
45.06.838 N • 121.15.384 W

Services:
none

Wapinitia is a Warm Springs Indian Word meaning "the edge of," suggesting the edge of a desert or a place where little grows, one reason the government gave this 300,000 acre reservation to the Warm Springs Tribes. Wapinitia was once an established community with several businesses, but only a few homes survive today.

Points of Interest

- **Wapinitia School** (*East Wapinitia Road at the crest of hill*) The 1899 school holds hay and farm implements.

- **Old House** (*corner of Reservation Road and East Wapinitia Road*) One of the remaining few.

Wapinitia School

Wapinitia to Simnasho

Distance:
12.0 miles

Directions:
From the corner of Reservation Road and East Wapinitia Road, continue south on Reservation Road.

Points En Route

(mileage from the intersection of Reservation Road and Wapinitia Road)

0.3 miles:
Wapinitia Cemetery (dates to 1889) and grange, circa 1910.

3.0 miles:
Crossing Paquet Creek, named for Frances Paquet, who opened a store in Wapinitia in 1876.

3.7 miles:
Entrance to the Warm Springs Indian Reservation.

6.5 miles:
From here Red Lake and Red Lake Cemetery are 0.4 miles to the left.

9.4 miles:
Great view of Mt. Jefferson (10,497 feet).

12.0 miles:
Simnasho

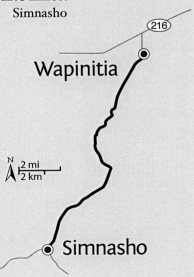

Simnasho

Elevation: 2,404 feet

Location:
44.58.388 N • 121.20.941 W

Services:
gas, food

The community's name comes from the Native American word for "bush of thorns," which grow abundantly in the area. The first school in Simnasho opened in 1882. Today the community consists of a convenience store and gas station, an old school, a beautiful but vacant old church, and a few homes. Simnasho was an important gathering place for the Warm Springs people, and today is the site of Lincoln's Pow-Wow, an event held every February.

Points of Interest

- **Old Church**
  (across from the store)
  Built in the early 1900s and thought to be Presbyterian.

- **Church Parsonage**
  (next to the church)
  A walkway once connected this to the church.

- **Simnasho School**
  (across from the convenience store)
  Now serving as the community center and police headquarters, this old school is located on Native American Highway 9.

old church

Simnasho to Warm Springs

Distance:
23.6 miles

Directions:
From the Intersection of Native American Highway 9 and Reservation Road, continue south on Reservation Road. (also known as Native American Highway 3)

Points En Route

(mileage from the intersection of Highway 9 and Reservation Road)

2.3 miles:
Simnasho Cemetery, dating to the late 1800s.

11.1 miles:
Warm Springs National Fish Hatchery.

12.3 miles:
Huge, beautiful rock outcropping.

13.3 miles:
Turn-off to Kah-Nee-Ta resort.

22.6 miles:
Warm Springs Industrial Park.

23.6 miles:
Junction with Highway 26.

23.6 miles:
Warm Springs

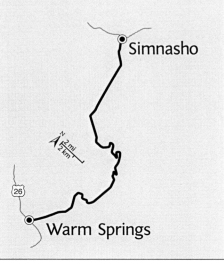

Warm Springs

Elevation: 1,496 feet

Location:
44.45.869 N • 121.16.056 W

Services:
gas, food, lodging

Warm Springs is located on an ancient Native American migration trail to the Columbia River. Between 1835 and 1855, Peter Skene Ogden, Nathaniel Wyeth, and John C. Fremont explored the area. The Warm Springs post office opened in 1873 and its first boarding school a year later. The Confederated Tribes of the Warm Springs – comprised of Wasco, Paiute and Warm Springs Indians – made this their community and cultural center in 1937.

Tribal Courthouse

Points of Interest

- **Deschutes River**
  (flows through town)
  Fly fishing only. A special permit is needed to fish on tribal waters.

- **Warm Springs Museum**
  (on Highway 26)
  Over 25,000 square feet of covered exhibits and history. Walking trails radiate from the magnificent structure.

- **Warm Springs Forest Products** *(Highway 26)*
  Owned and operated by Warm Springs Tribal members.

- **Warm Springs State Park**
  (on Highway 26)
  Pit toilets and boat launch.

- **Old Store**
  (2130 Warm Springs Street)
  This building housed the first general mercantile store in town.

- **Skate Park** *(Hollywood Street)*
  Near the community center and adjacent to the city park, the new skate park has a picnic area and restrooms.

- **Fire House**
  (2127 Warm Springs Avenue)
  The brick building once held the community's fire-fighting equipment, beginning with a horse drawn pumper.

- **Shaker Church** *(Shittike Road)*
  Built in 1910 with a bell tower.

- **Tribal Courthouse**
  (between Paiute and Wasco)
  Built in the 1870s, it was the Indian Agency Building before becoming the Tribal Courthouse.

- **Old School and Dormitories**
  (110 Wasco)
  The first schools dated to the 1870s, but the brick buildings that still stand were constructed after the treaty of 1935, when the Confederated Tribal Council formed.

- **Boarding House** *(1102 Wasco)*
  Built in the early 1900s and closed for more than two decades.

- **Warm Springs Cemetery**
  (Tenino Road)
  0.5 miles on Tenino Road. Dates to the 1870s.

- **Bruno Cemetery**
  (0.5 miles south on Tenino Road)
  Dates to the 1870s.

Warm Springs Museum

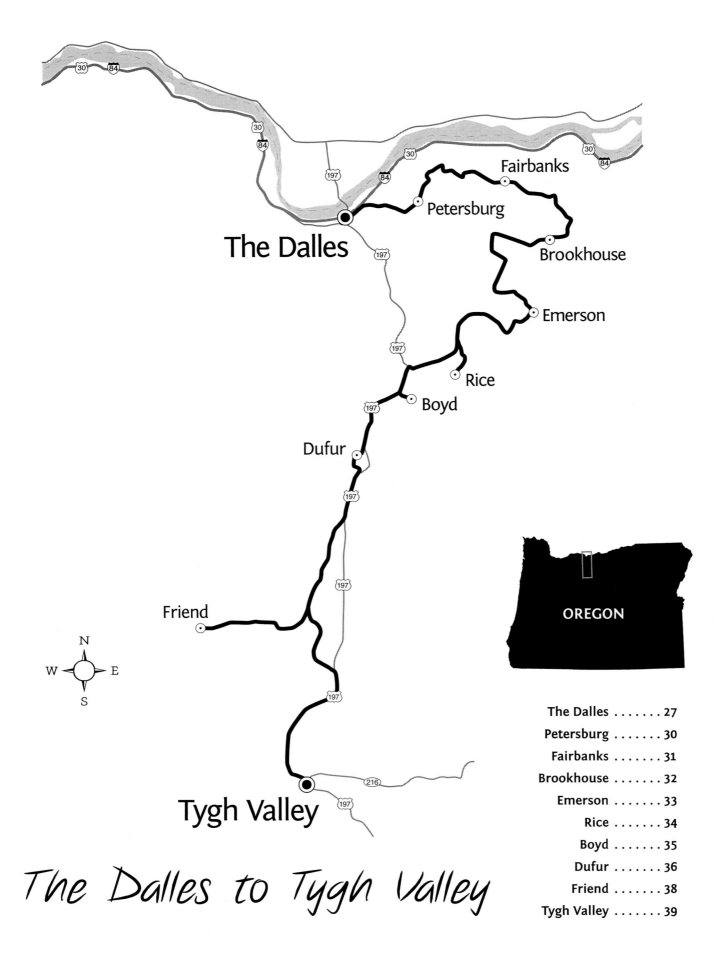

OREGON

The Dalles to Tygh Valley

Finding a Friend Near Dufur

The Dalles to Tygh Valley (47 miles)

Eons before the first settlers arrived in the Northwest, long before even the first Native Americans arrived, north-central Oregon was bursting with volcanic activity. The Cascade Range was formed during the Eocene Period, 40 million years ago, and most recent major eruptions occurred in the Miocene Period, 15 million years ago. These last eruptions created the major mountains in the Northwest, including Mount Hood. As many as 300 eruptions occurred during the Pleistocene Period, when volcanic magma formed lava walls as thick as 500 feet in central Oregon and Washington. Then, during the Ice Age, 13,000 to 16,000 years ago, the Missoula Floods carved the current Columbia River channel and eroded these walls.

As far as the area's human history is concerned, The Dalles once marked the end of the early overland Oregon Trail, and Wasco County, formed in 1854 as the nation's largest county, sprawled for more than 130,000 square miles across the Northwest and all the way to the Rocky Mountains. Now The Dalles serves as the starting point for an excursion to Tygh Valley, which crosses significant points along the Oregon Trail. It passes through wheat fields, past wind generators and into the remains of communities whose existence ceased when the railroad bypassed their isolated depots. Along the way, the geography and habitat change significantly from the Columbia Gorge, up the plateau, and toward the edge of the Cascades.

the road between Dufur and Friend

The Dalles

Elevation: 109 feet

Location:
45.36.147 N • 121.10.977 W

Services:
gas, food, lodging, B&B

The Dalles' name originates from the French "dalle," which means trenchstone, and relates to the massive basalt rock formations that narrow at The Dalles on the Columbia, resembling gutters. Erected on an 1805 Lewis and Clark campsite, Fort The Dalles is one of Oregon's oldest communities, with the post office opening in 1851. It became the Wasco County seat in 1854 and was officially incorporated in 1857. This mid-Columbia trade center is considered the end of the overland Oregon Trail. From 1843 until 1846, years before the Barlow Trail was constructed, the earliest pioneers left their wagons at Crates Point, near the Columbia Gorge Discovery Center, and took barges or homemade rafts down the perilous, rough and tumble Columbia River, west to the Willamette River. Once constructed, the Barlow Trail offered pioneers an option of continued wagon travel over the treacherous Laurel Hill descent to Oregon City. Obtain a walking tour of The Dalles' historic buildings from the Chamber of Commerce or most local merchants.

Lone Pine Village with The Dalles Dam behind

Points of Interest

- **Waldron Drug Store**
  (*1st and Washington*)
  While this rebuilt 1867 drug store, emporium and former Masonic Lodge still stands, a devastating fire in 1878 took the life of owner H.J. Waldron. Poet Walt Whitman stayed here when it was a boarding house.

- **Telegraph Building**
  (*between 1st and 2nd on Washington*)
  Built in 1880.

- **Lemke's Saloon** (*119 2nd*)
  Constructed in the early 1900s and now home to the Oregon Equipment Company.

- **Granada Theater**
  (*2nd and Union*)
  After opening in 1928, this was the first theater west of the Mississippi to show "talkies."

Surgeon's Quarters at Fort The Dalles

- **Chinese Building** (*210 East 1st*)
Once the center of the town's Chinese community.

- **Gayer Building** (*300 East 2nd*)
The 1879 building, now a jewelry store, housed the town's first bank.

- **Pioneer Building** (*301 East 2nd*)
One of Oregon's first mercantiles, opening in 1860.

Moody-Patrick House

- **Klindt's Booksellers**
(*315 East 2nd*)
Its 1870 beginning makes this the oldest continuously operating bookstore in Oregon.

- **Pease Department Store**
(*320 East 2nd*)
The original early 1870s store is now home to Klindt's Booksellers and an office supply outlet.

- **Turner Furniture** (*624 East 2nd*)
The Wasco Hotel until the 1950s, this building has also been a brothel, saloon, restaurant and stage stop.

- **U.S. Mint Building**
(*710 East 2nd*)
Despite the amounts of gold mined in Oregon during the 1860s, the mint was never commissioned and never struck a coin. Home to US Cellular today.

- **Buchler Building** (*906 East 2nd*)
Former home of the Columbia Brewery, which closed in 1915.

- **The Dalles Chamber of Commerce** (*404 West 2nd*)
Here you can obtain walking-tour information about the historic community.

- **First Wasco County Courthouse** (*410 West 2nd*)
The first courthouse was built in 1859, the year of Oregon's statehood, to serve as the center of government for the largest county in the history of the United States.

- **Baldwin's Saloon**
(*205 Court*)
First a saloon and then a saddle shop and now back in the bar business. Original paintings, including landscapes and nudes, line the walls.

- **I.O.O.F Lodge**
(*2nd and Laughlin*)
First built in 1856, this building burned in 1891 and again in 1914. It was rebuilt in 1915.

- **Sunshine Biscuit Company**
(*2nd and Taylor*)
Opened in 1869.

- **Second Wasco County Courthouse** (*105 3rd*)
Constructed in 1881, the building now houses a Masonic Lodge and Smith-Calloway Funeral Home.

- **St. Peter's Catholic Church**
(*3rd and Liberty*)
Erected in 1897, this church with a 176-foot steeple was spared from demolition in 1971. It houses an 1880 collapsible pump organ, tin ceilings, Italian marble altars, and a carved Madonna (circa 1850) that was the prow of a ship that sailed around Cape Horn.

- **Basalt Rock Wall** (*West 3rd between Trevitt and West 4th*)
Built by Italian immigrants.

- **Sinott House** (*4th and Lincoln*)
Constructed in 1868.

First Wasco County Courthouse

The Dalles

Points of Interest (continued)

- **Pentland House**
  (*4th and Lincoln*)
  Built in 1880.

- **Third Wasco County
  Courthouse** (*509 Washington*)
  Build in 1912.

- **Old Bank** (*515 Liberty*)
  One of the city's first banks is
  now a restaurant.

- **French House** (*550 Liberty*)
  1865 construction.

- **The Dalles City Park**
  (*6th and Union*)
  A boulder here is inscribed "End
  of the Oregon Trail, 1843-1906."

- **Old St. Paul's Episcopal
  Church** (*601 Union*)
  Built in 1875, this once held a
  museum.

Petland Home and Sinnott House

- **Fort Dalles** (*15th and Garrison*)
  Built in 1850 and abandoned in
  1867, the fort still has a few of
  its original buildings, including
  the 1856 Gardener's Cottage,
  which was moved from the
  middle of what is now the high
  school football field, and the
  1859 Surgeon's Quarters, which
  has been a museum since 1905,
  making it the oldest in Oregon.

- **Hole in the Rock**
  (*on the grounds of the Shilo Inn Suites
  at 3223 Bret Clodfelter Way – also
  knows as Seufert Park Road*)
  Native American legend states
  that if the hole in the rock were
  naturally filled with dirt, the
  ever-present winds would stop
  blowing.

- **Lone Pine Village**
  (*adjacent to the Shilo Inn Suites*)
  Beginning in 1896, a shaker
  community once stood here,
  encircling a now gone pine tree.

- **The Dalles Dam**
  (*viewed from Lone Pine Village*)
  Starting in 1957, this hydroelectric
  dam slowed the flow of the
  mighty Columbia River.

- **The Dalles Murals:**
  Located throughout the historic
  downtown, these works of art
  illustrate significant events in
  Oregon's history.

- **Pioneer Cemetery**
  (*400 block of Scenic Drive*)
  Dates to the 1850s.

- **Sorosis Park** (*on Scenic Drive*)
  Sitting high above the Columbia,
  the park offers a fitness course,
  picnic area, rose garden,
  restrooms, playground, Veterans
  Memorial, and beautiful views of
  the river, mountains, and city.

- **Columbia Gorge Discovery
  Center and Wasco County
  Historical Society**
  (*500 Discovery Drive*)
  This 26,500-square foot center
  describes both the natural and
  human history of the Columbia
  Gorge. Nearby is Crates Point,
  where pioneers began their raft
  trips down the Columbia to the
  Willamette.

The Dalles to Petersburg

Distance:
4.0 miles

Directions:
From the Shilo Inn at the intersection of Highway 197 and Lone Pine Drive, turn left onto Highway 197 and travel south, crossing Interstate 84 and the railroad tracks.

Points En Route

(mileage from the Shiloh Inn)

0.3 miles:
Crossroads of Highway 197 and Highway 30. Turn right and head west.

0.5 miles:
Intersection with SE Frontage Road. Turn right and travel east.

2.0 miles:
Interesting metal structure in the distance to the left. There are many orchards between The Dalles and Petersburg.

3.7 miles:
Intersection with Fifteen Mile Road. Turn left.

4.0 miles:
Petersburg

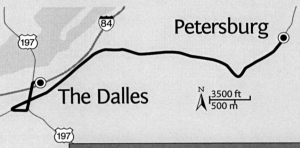

Petersburg

Elevation: 304 feet

Location:
45.36.560 N • 121.04.739 W

Services:
none

Established in 1905, Petersburg was named after Peter Strohler, a homesteader who lived on Fifteen Mile Creek. The post office opened in 1906 and closed in 1940, seven years after the railroad tracks were removed. Little remains of the community except the old school and a few homes.

Points of Interest

- **Old Petersburg School**
  (on Fifteen Mile Road)
  The original 1910 school has been replaced with a modern brick building.

- **Petersburg Cemetery**
  (near the juncture of Eightmile Road and Fifteen Mile Road)
  This pioneer cemetery dates to the early 1900s.

Old Petersburg School

Petersburg to Fairbanks

Distance:
5.5 miles

Directions:
From the old Petersburg School, proceed east on the Petersburg-Fairbanks Road.

Points En Route

(mileage from the old Petersburg School)

0.1 miles:
The new Petersburg School is part of The Dalles School District.

2.1 miles:
Marsh area, located near Fifteen Mile Creek. Look for chukar, quail and grouse.

4.5 miles:
One of the earlier homes in the Fairbanks area, constructed in the early 1900s.

5.5 miles:
Fairbanks

Fairbanks

Elevation: 499 feet

Location:
45.37.455 N • 121.00.123 W

Services:
none

Fairbanks got its start on the banks of Fifteen Mile Creek when the railroad laid track here. The community was named for United States Vice-President Charles Fairbanks, who served under Theodore Roosevelt at the time the post office opened in 1905. The post office operated a short four years before closing. The railroad tracks were removed during the Depression in the 1930s, ending commercial shipping and reducing the population of the community. A few farmhouses and the old schoolhouse are all that remain of Fairbanks. There is a monument, near the entrance to the old school, commemorating the route that many pioneers traveled.

Points of Interest

- **Fairbanks School** *(near the creek)*
  Built in 1907, the school closed in 1938 and students were bussed to nearby Petersburg.

monument along the road to Fairbanks where it crosses the Oregon Trail

Fairbanks School

Brookhouse

Elevation: 699 feet

Location:
45.35.263 N • 120.57.830 W

Services:
none

Named for the pioneer settlers who once lived near the brook, the community never had a post office or a school. Wheat farming and cattle ranching have long provided the economic base for the area's sparse population.

old hay barn along the road to Brookhouse

Fairbanks to Brookhouse

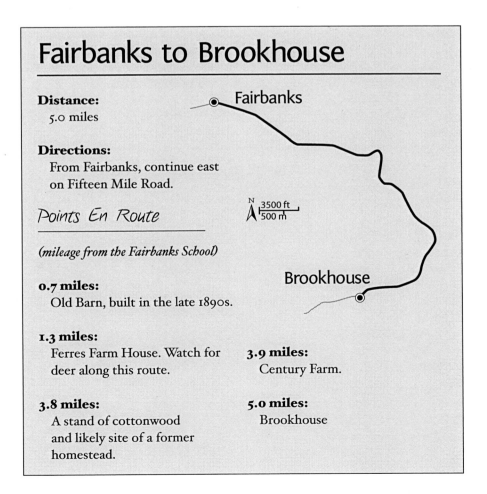

Distance:
5.0 miles

Directions:
From Fairbanks, continue east on Fifteen Mile Road.

Points En Route

(mileage from the Fairbanks School)

0.7 miles:
Old Barn, built in the late 1890s.

1.3 miles:
Ferres Farm House. Watch for deer along this route.

3.8 miles:
A stand of cottonwood and likely site of a former homestead.

3.9 miles:
Century Farm.

5.0 miles:
Brookhouse

the view into Emerson

Emerson

Elevation: 841 feet

Location:

45.32.719 N • 120.58.785 W

Services:

Named for an 1884 settler, Emerson was an important rail stop on the Great Southern Railroad. The tracks were removed in the 1930s, ending Emerson's importance as a shipping terminus.

Points of Interest

- **The old Great Southern Railroad Depot and Loading Dock**
  Along with one house, the large train depot and shipping area still stands in the midst of grain fields. One can only imagine the tracks that paralleled this large shipping depot. Look for Fifteen Mile Creek near the farmhouse.

Brookhouse to Emerson

Distance:

9.4 miles

Directions:

From Brookhouse, continue south on Fifteen Mile Road.

Points En Route

(mileage from Fifteen Mile Road and Kelly Cut-off Road intersection)

3.0 miles:

Desilting Basin to the right. A project to improve water quality in the area.

3.7 miles:

Old farmhouse, complete with barn, windmill and outbuildings.

4.5 miles:

More windmills, used to pump water.

4.7 miles:

Still more windmills.

5.0 miles:

Fifteen Mile Road becomes Roberts Market Road and intersects with Emerson-Roberts Road. Turn right onto Emerson-Roberts Road. Pavement turns to nicely maintained four-miles of gravel.

6.3 miles:

The 1890s Douglas Hill School, a one-room structure, sits weathered, abandoned and surrounded by hay fields.

8.9 miles:

Old barn and windmill.

9.1 miles:

Intersection with Wrentham Cut-Off Road. Turn right, continuing on Emerson-Roberts Road.

9.4 miles:

Emerson

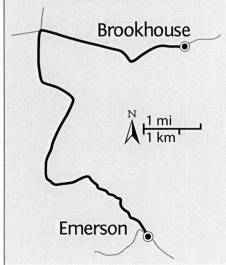

Brookhouse

N

1 mi

1 km

Emerson

Douglas Hill School

Emerson to Rice

Distance:
5.2 miles

Directions:
From the depot, return to Emerson-Wrentham Road.

Points En Route

(mileage from the Great Southern Railroad Depot)

0.2 mile:
Intersection with Emerson-Wrentham Cut-off Road. Turn right and go toward Rice.

1.3 miles:
Pavement returns at the intersection of Wrentham Cut-off Road and Wrentham Road. Turn right onto Wrentham Road.

2.0 miles:
Site of Wrentham, named for a pioneer family that hailed from Wrentham, New York. A post office was established in 1900 and was closed in 1916. At the intersection of Wrentham Road and Emerson Loop Road, turn left onto Emerson Loop Road.

2.4 miles:
Frequently photographed Charlie Nelson homestead.

2.8 miles:
Old homestead with outbuildings and old cherry trees.

3.5 miles:
Intersection of Emerson Loop Road and Ward Road. Turn left on Ward Road.

3.7 miles:
Century Farm.

4.1 miles:
Veer left onto Fax Road, which turns into a well-maintained gravel road. Look for raptors soaring above the cherry orchards.

5.2 miles:
Rice

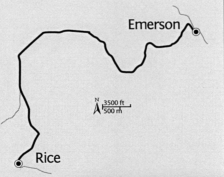

Rice

Elevation: 1,017 feet

Location:
45.30.702 N • 121.02.238 W

Services:
none

Rice was named for early settler and wheat farmer Horace Rice, who came to the area in the 1860s and was one of the first to raise wheat on this Wasco County plateau. The town almost disappeared after the railroad tracks and depot were removed in the 1930s. Today, wheat fields surround scores of recently planted cherry trees, as do tall fences that keep deer from eating fruit, leaves and bark.

Points of Interest

- **Old Grain Storage Bins**
  These buildings once stored large amounts of grain, waiting to be loaded onto rail cars.

- **Old Livestock Corral**
  Used to pen cattle before they were loaded onto rail cars and processed in The Dalles.

barn in Rice

Charlie Nelson Homestead

Distance:
    5.6 miles

Directions:
    From Rice; backtrack on Fax Road to Ward Road.

Points En Route

(mileage from the grain storage buildings)

1.1 miles:
    Turn left onto Ward Road.

3.8 miles:
    At the intersection of Ward Road and Highway 197, turn left toward Dufur.

4.8 miles:
    Turn left onto Boyd Loop Road.

5.6 miles:
    Boyd

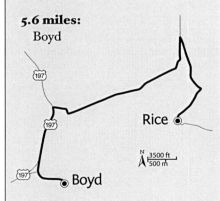

Boyd

Elevation: 1,213 feet

Location:
45.29.269 N • 121.05.017 W

Services:
none

A living ghost town, Boyd was settled in the 1880s as a stopover for miners who were heading to the southern Oregon gold fields. The post office opened in 1884. The town was named after early settler and flourmill owner-operator John Boyd. A store, mill and hotel are memories of this former community. A few people still reside among the abandoned homes.

Points of Interest

- **Wooden grain elevator**
  (next to the creek)
  The capacity of this storage unit is estimated at more than 100,000 bushels.

wooden grain elevator

Distance:
4.2 miles

Directions:
From Boyd, backtrack on Boyd Loop Road to Highway 197 and then turn right.

Points En Route

(mileage from the bridge over Fifteen Mile Creek on Boyd Loop Road)

0.8 miles:
Intersection with Highway 197. Turn right.

2.8 miles:
Boyd Cemetery, dating to the 1890s.

4.0 miles:
Turn right, to Dufur.

4.2 miles:
Dufur

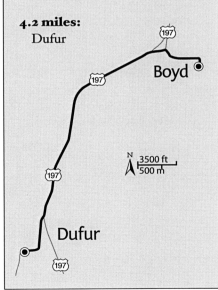

Dufur

Elevation: 1,304 feet

Location:
45.27.096 N • 121.07.864 W

Services:
gas, food, B&B, RV Park

First known as Fifteen Mile Crossing and settled as early as 1852, Dufur was once a stop along the Barlow Trail. About 1863, a hotel and roadhouse were built near Fifteen Mile Creek, close to the current location of the Dufur Museum. The post office opened in 1878 and the town, named for one of the pioneer brothers who raised sheep near the present downtown area, was incorporated in 1893. In 1907, Dufur residents were excited about the prospect of discovering oil near town, but after three years with no wells, further efforts were discontinued. In the 1910s, more than 400 acres of apple trees covered the hills, but by the late 1930s a lack of water for raising quality apples and the high price that farmers received for their grain put an end to fruit growing. Today the community, the second largest in Wasco County with a population of just over 600, is know for its annual steam-threshing event that in August pays homage to the early days of grain harvesting. Main Street is the actual route of the Oregon Trail.

Balch Hotel

Points of Interest

- **Balch Hotel** (*Main Street*)
  The 1907 Hotel was recently remodeled and converted into a bed and breakfast.

- **Fort Dufur Site**
  (*Main and Hogan's Alley*)
  The original fort was built here in 1884. It was abandoned in the 1890s, quickly fell into a state of disrepair, and was finally demolished in the early 1900s. Located here today are RV sites and a park.

- **Dufur Tavern** (*Main Street*)
  The tavern stands on the site of the 1852 Fifteen Mile House, a stage stop and public house on the Oregon Trail.

- **Dufur Museum**
  (*on Main Street near the creek*)
  The old building was a pioneer home, relocated from Friend, twelve miles to the southwest. The 1851 wagon-cookhouse is a pride of the museum.

Dufur

Points of Interest (continued)

Dufur Museum and Endersby School

- **Endersby School**
  (*Main, behind the museum*)
  The school, moved from
  Endersby, six miles north, served
  students from 1892 to 1935. The
  old "two-hole" came with the
  school when it was moved to its
  present location in 1992.

- **Dufur House**
  (*Green house on 1st Avenue*)
  The 1872 home of Andrew Dufur,
  sheep rancher and town founder.

- **Kramer's Market** (*Main and 1st*)
  Since 1906 five generations
  of Kraemer's have owned and
  operated the store, which is
  famous for its sausage. Old spice
  tins, scales, and cash registers
  are displayed around the store.
  Handwritten charge account books
  are still used to record the grocery
  orders of community members.

- **Dufur Grange** (*Main and 5th*)
  A monthly bluegrass music
  performance site. Players come
  from all around for a chance to
  play at the hall.

- **Dufur Cemetery** (*north of town*)
  Dates to 1869, initially as the
  IOOF Cemetery.

- **Annabelle Dufur Home**
  (*1.7 miles from Dufur on Dufur
  Valley Road*)
  Built in 1880, this was the home
  of Annabelle Dufur, daughter of
  the town founder.

- **Ramsey Hall**
  (*4.8 miles from Dufur on Dufur
  Valley Road*)
  The old grange and a few homes
  are what is left of this old
  community that was bypassed by
  the railroad.

Dufur to Friend

Distance:
12.0 miles

Directions:
In Dufur, go south on Main
Street, past the Balch Hotel to the
intersection of Dufur Valley Road
and Dufur Bypass Road. Turn left
onto Bypass Road.

Points En Route

(*mileage from the intersection of Dufur
Valley Road and Dufur Bypass Road*)

0.6 miles:
Intersection with Highway 97.
Turn right.

2.4 miles:
Turn right onto Dufur Gap
Road.

3.3 miles:
Canyon Creek Game Farm.
Note the protective netting over
the game pens.

3.4 miles:
Elevation 1,733 feet.

6.0 miles:
Elevation 2,021 feet.

6.9 miles:
Turn right onto Friend Road.

8.4 miles:
Elevation 2,464 feet. Excellent
view of the Cascades.

8.7 miles:
Intersection of Friend Road and
Kingsley Road. Stay on Friend
Road. Kingsley Road leads to
the site of Kingsley, a farming
settlement that had its own
post office from 1893 until 1927.
Kingsley was named in honor of
author and cleric, Charles Kingsley.

9.2 miles:
Wilson house, home to one of the
early settlers in the Kingsley area.

10.8 miles:
Note change in vegetation, with
pine and oak trees growing in
abundance.

12.0 miles:
Friend (look for a road sign that
reads 80387). Turn right into the
remains of the small community.

Friend

Elevation: 2,436 feet

Location:
45.20.733 N • 121.15.843 W

Services:
none

This living ghost town was named for George Friend, pioneer homesteader. The post office opened in 1903 and was housed in the general store. Besides the school and the store, which still stand, Friend boasted two churches, a sawmill, blacksmith shop, land office, a tinner, insurance, barber and pool hall. The community declined when the railroad went into bankruptcy during the Great Depression.

Mt. Hood from outside Friend

Points of Interest

- **Friend General Store**
  (several hundred yards down Road 80387)
  The general store is the only building remaining from a series of businesses that once lined the street.

- **T.C. Murray's General Store**
  (Friend Road and Heberlein)
  A brick-lined vault standing in the field to the left of the road is all that remains of Murray's store.

- **Friend School** *(intersection of Clark Mill Road and Friend Road)*
  Travel 0.6 miles down Friend Road to view the school. Friend school served students from 1905 until 1961.

- **Friend Cemetery**
  (1.1 miles on Clark Mill Road)
  From the school, proceed up Clark Mill Road to the 1885 cemetery.

Friend General Store

Friend to Tygh Valley

Distance:
  14.7 miles

Directions:
  From road 80387, return east on
  Friend Road.

Points En Route

*(mileage from road 80387 and Friend
Road)*

5.1 miles:
  Turn right onto Dufur Gap
  Road.

7.6 miles:
  Summit of Tygh Ridge, elevation
  2647 feet.

8.4 miles:
  Turn right and travel south on
  Highway 197.

13.6 miles:
  Junction with the Fairgrounds;
  Hunt Park in the distance.

14.5 miles:
  Proceed right onto Tygh Valley
  Road, which follows the old
  Barlow Trail.

14.7 miles:
  Tygh Valley

Tygh Valley

Elevation: 1,138 feet

Location:
45.14.860 N • 121.10.378 W

Services:
gas, food, RV Park and camping

Tygh Valley, nestled at the base of 3,000 foot-high Tygh Ridge and located on the Old Barlow Trail, was once a winter hunting grounds for the Tyghee people, a Chinook tribe. In their language, the word *Tyghee* means "peaceful." The area's first settlers, the Butler brothers, arrived in the 1850s. Daniel Butler, the eldest brother, moved to The Dalles and was the first justice of the peace in Wasco County. He went on to become a deputy sheriff. After leaving The Dalles area in 1865, he moved permanently to Tygh Valley, where he built and ran a trading post. The community opened its post office in 1873 and incorporated in 1892. The economy once thrived on timber and is slowly recovering via farming and tourism. Pioneer wagon ruts are still visible in several places along the hillsides.

Points of Interest

- **Tygh Valley General Store**
  (downtown on Tygh Valley Road)
  Old photos and pictures from
  the community's early days are
  displayed on the walls of this
  wooden-floored building.

- **Oldest homes in Tygh Valley**
  *(below the store and adjacent to the
  river, on either side of the highway)*
  Both houses date to the 1880s.

Tygh Valley General Store

- **IOOF Cemetery**
  (Tygh Valley Road)
  Dates to the 1880s.

- **Native American Rodeo Grounds** *(across highway 197)*
  Rodeo grounds for the annual Native American summer event.

- **Tygh Valley School** *(Havens Street and Tygh Valley Road)*
  The main part of the school was built in 1899 and now serves as the community center.

- **Tygh Valley Cemetery**
  (0.9 miles south on Tygh Valley Road)
  Dates to the 1880s.

- **White River Falls State Park** *(4 miles south and west off of Highway 216)*
  The site of a 1880s gristmill and 1900-1939 hydroelectric station, both located near the dramatic falls. The Mill's foundations are still present as is the aqueduct used to divert water to the old powerhouse.

- **Sherar's Bridge** *(7.7 miles east of Tygh Valley on Highway 216)*
  This was a Native American fishing grounds and pioneer crossing. Peter Skene Ogden first crossed this point in 1826. In 1860 John Todd built the first bridge here, selling it to Joseph Sherar in 1871. Sherar operated the bridge in the 1890s, charging tolls to wagon trains using the Barlow Cut-off.

old home in Tygh Valley

White River Falls

Sherar's Grade

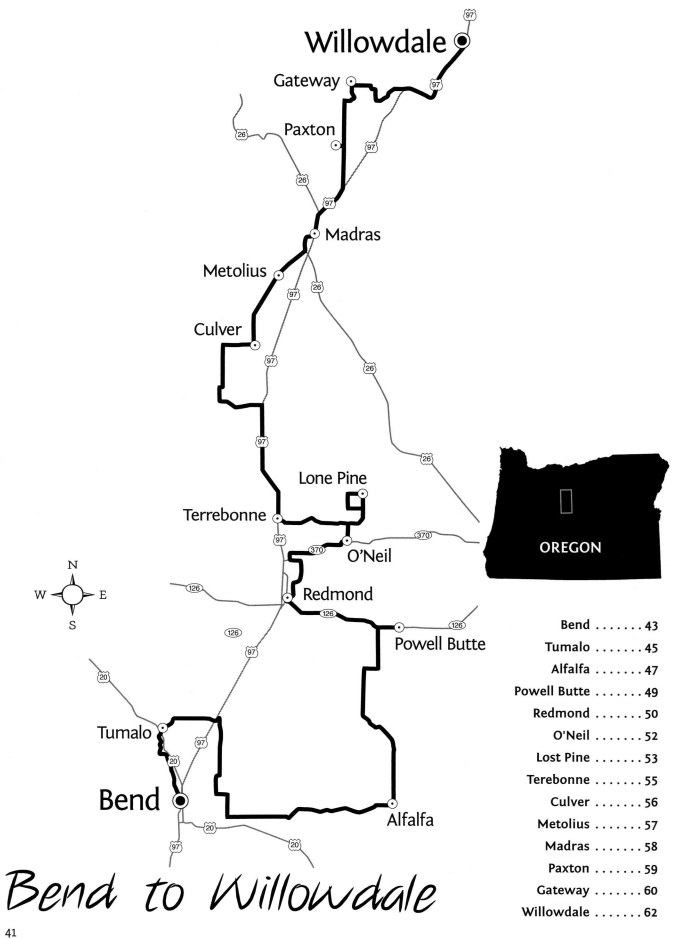

Willowdale

Gateway

Paxton

Madras

Metolius

Culver

Lone Pine

Terrebonne

O'Neil

Redmond

Powell Butte

Tumalo

Bend

Alfalfa

OREGON

N
W E
S

Bend to Willowdale

Stage Stops and Pioneer Graves

Bend to Willowdale (116 miles)

Beginning in the region's population center of Bend, this tour connects fourteen towns and small communities, including some of Oregon's youngest. Prior to the 1900s, some of these communities existed only as stage stops until construction of roads, railroads, irrigation canals, and deep wells all hastened the development of the region.

Today, this is the fastest growing area in the state, with the population of the Bend-Redmond area quadrupling in recent decades. In addition, its approximately 280 days of sunshine a year make this high desert, forested area a popular gateway for year-round recreation.

the road between Paxton and Gateway

Bend

Elevation: 3,550 feet

Location:
44.03.472 N • 121.18.982 W

Services:
gas, food, lodging, B&B

Although it was first known as Farewell Bend when it was a wagon crossing on the Deschutes River along a spur of the Oregon Trail – The Free Emigrant Road – the post office opened in 1886 as "Bend" because Farewell Bend already existed on the Snake River along the Oregon-Idaho border. Beginning in 1910, the railroad, a hydroelectric plant, irrigation canals, and telephone service all arrived here within four years. Bend, one of the fastest growing communities in the Northwest, celebrated its 100th birthday as a city in 2005. John Todd, for whom Todd Lake is named, was the first settler in the area and farmed near the famous bend in the river.

Reid School

Points of Interest

- **Drake Park** (*on Deschutes River near old Bend City Center*)
Named after the founder of the Pilot Butte Development Company, who brought irrigation canals and water to this part of the state. The town's first school, built in 1881, once stood in the park.

- **Bend Fire Station** (*5 NW Minnesota*)
This 1920 building constructed of locally made bricks was Bend's first Fire Station, and once housed two fire-fighting vehicles and one employee.

- **Sather House** (*7 NW Tumalo*)
Evan Sather, Bend's first professional photographer, built this home in 1911. Sather's downtown photography studio was located at 916 NW Wall.

- **O'Kane Building** (*115 Oregon*)
Built of concrete in 1916 to withstand fires that plagued many turn of the century businesses.

- **Reid School** (*129 Idaho*)
Completed in 1914, the old school now houses the Deschutes County Historical Society.

- **McCann House** (*440 NW Congress*)
The first manager of the Shevlin-Hixon Lumber Company built this Georgian Revival house in 1916.

Bend Train Depot

- **Bend Bulletin** (*624 Franklin*)
  The old newspaper building was built in 1912.

H. E. Allen House

- **Putnam House**
  (*606 NW Congress*)
  Built in 1911, this was home to G.P. Putnam, the New York publishing company heir and husband to Amelia Earhart. Putnam owned and operated the local paper for several years before heading back to New York to run the family's publishing business.

- **Lara House** (*640 NW Congress*)
  Now a bed and breakfast establishment, this lovely Craftsman-style house belonged to A.M. Lara, who owned Bend's first mercantile store.

- **Homer Building**
  (*704 NW Georgia*)
  Mercantile store built of concrete blocks in 1916.

- **Liberty Theater** (*849 NW Wall*)
  The oldest movie theater in Bend, built in 1917, seats 500.

- **Bend Hardware** (*856 NW Bond*)
  Home to the first hardware store in town, the two-story, 1918 building was one of the first to be constructed of brick.

- **Downing Hotel** (*1033 NW Bond*)
  First opened its doors in 1919.

- **Pine Tree Tavern**
  (*967 NW Brooks*)
  The tavern, uniquely constructed around a Pine Tree, opened in 1936.

- **Cashman's Store**
  (*1001 NW Wall*)
  This retail location once housed Buster Brown Shoes, several clothing shops, a pool hall, and an office supply store.

- **Bend Amateur Athletic Club**
  (*Wall and Idaho*)
  Constructed in 1918, this building has been used as a hospital as well as a recreation and community center.

- **Tucker Building**
  (*200 NW Greenwood*)
  Bend's second Blacksmith Shop is now home to the Deschutes County Law Library.

- **Blacksmith Shop**
  (*211 NW Greenwood*)
  After closing in 1973, this 1923 shop has been converted to the Blacksmith Restaurant.

- **Wright Hotel**
  (*215 NW Greenwood*)
  This 1911 hotel was once one of Bend's finest.

- **Williamson House**
  (*390 NW Greenwood*)
  Bend's first car dealer once owned this 1915 home.

- **Pilot Butte and Greenwood Cemeteries** (*off Greenwood near Pilot Butte*)
  Both cemeteries, which share boundaries, date to the early 1900s.

- **Pilot Butte State Park**
  (*from intersection of Highways 97 and 20, go east 0.9 miles on Highway 20, also known as Greenwood Avenue*)
  At an elevation of 4,139 feet, the butte stands more than 500 feet higher than the downtown area.

- **High Desert Museum** (*5.5 miles south of Bend on Highway 97*)
  The museum opened in 1982 with attractions for all ages.

Old Mill

Bend to Tumalo

Distance:
5.3 miles

Directions:
Go north on Highway 97 to the Bend River Mall. Turn west onto O.B. Riley Road.

Points En Route

(mileage from the intersection of Highway 97 and O.B. Riley Road)

0.4 miles:
High Desert Management Unit Office.

1.0 miles:
Waldorf School, a private, non-traditional school.

3.4 miles:
Great vistas of Cascade peaks.

3.9 miles:
Tumalo State Park. Camp, picnic, fish, swim, hike and raft.

5.2 miles:
Intersection with Highway 20. Cross the highway, continuing north into Tumalo.

5.3 miles:
Tumalo

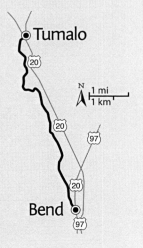

Tumalo

Elevation: 3,173 feet

Location:
44.08.933 N • 121.19.853 W

Services:
gas, food

The community was originally named Laidlaw in 1904 after W.A. Laidlaw, an early land speculator and developer. Around 1911 the name changed to *Tumalo* from the Klamath Indian word meaning "wild plum" – once plentiful in the area – and for the irrigation project, completed in 1915, that brought water to this part of the high desert.

Points of Interest

- **Laidlaw Bank and Trust Building** *(5th and Cook)*
  Built in 1905, the building was one of the first constructed in the new community. It now houses the headquarters for the Tumalo Irrigation District. Photos of the early irrigation canal construction can be seen through the windows. The diversion canals were completed in 1915.

- **Tumalo Community Church** *(64671 Bruce Street)*
  The oldest church in Deschutes County, the 1907 nondenominational worship center rings its cast iron bell every Sunday. The church organ came "'round the horn" and is one of only three similar instruments that exist today.

- **Tumalo Grange** *(adjacent to the church at 64671 Bruce)*
  Built in 1911, now a hall for the church.

- **Old homes** *(scattered through town)*
  Tumalo has several houses dating to the 1910s.

Laidlaw Bank and Trust Building

Tumalo Community Church

Tumalo to Alfalfa

Distance:
  22.2 miles

Directions:
  From Tumalo, go north on Tumalo Road, also called Tumalo-Deschutes Highway.

Points En Route

(mileage from the intersection of Cook Avenue and Tumalo Road)

0.1 miles:
  Crossing the Deschutes River.

1.1 miles:
  Deschutes River Ranch.

1.7 miles:
  Intersection with Bend/Redmond Highway. Continue straight on Tumalo Road.

3.4 miles:
  View of the Three Sisters Mountains.

3.8 miles:
  The Tumalo/Deschutes Highway crosses over Highway 97. This is the site of the community once called Deschutes Junction.

3.9 miles:
  Turn left, staying on the Tumalo-Deschutes Highway.

4.1 miles:
  Turn right onto Deschutes Market Road and proceed south.

4.3 miles:
  Railroad tracks and rough crossing.

7.7 miles:
  Note piles of rocks, stacked by farmers clearing fields.

8.0 miles:
  Turn right, staying on Deschutes Market Road.

8.7 miles:
  A large building, possibly a former grange or gym, marks the site of the former community of Butler.

9.5 miles:
  Turn left onto Butler Market Road.

10.3 miles:
  Turn right onto Hamby Road.

11.3 miles:
  Buckingham School, part of the Bend School District.

11.8 miles:
  Turn left onto Neff Road.

12.0 miles:
  Big Sky Park and Youth Sports Complex.

12.8 miles:
  Stop sign. Stay on Neff Road. There are many traffic fatality memorials on this stretch of road.

13.7 miles:
  At the stop sign, cross Powell Butte Highway and continue east as Neff Road becomes Alfalfa Market Road.

14.0 miles:
  Car bodies litter a field.

22.2 miles:
  Alfalfa

Tumalo

20 97

97

20

20

Alfalfa

N 2 mi
   2 km

Alfalfa Market Road at Dobbs Road

46

Alfalfa

Elevation: 3,395 feet

Location:
44.04.692 N • 121.02.820 W

Services:
gas, food

A tree-lined farmhouse identifies the beginning of Alfalfa, which stretches more than 1.5 miles and was named for the area's dominant crop. Its post office opened in 1912 but closed just ten years later. Farming took hold when the irrigation canals were completed. Alfalfa is also a jumping-off point to recreation areas at Brownlee Dam, Prineville Reservoir, and Crooked Finger Canyon.

Alfalfa Store

Points of Interest

(mileage from the Alfalfa Community Market)

- **Johnson Ranch Road** *(1.0 miles)*
  Intersection with Johnson Ranch Road.

- **Alfalfa Church** *(1.1 miles east on Alfalfa Market Road)*
  Over seventy years old.

- **Alfalfa Community Center** *(1.3 miles)*
  Formerly the Alfalfa Grange.

- **Alfalfa Store** *(1.4 miles east on Alfalfa Market Road)*
  Built in 1950.

- **Alfalfa School** *(1.5 miles east on Alfalfa Market Road)*
  Now a private home with a playground.

- **Lost Pioneer Grave**
  (for hikers or 4-wheel drive rigs only)
  The shallow grave, revealing the body of an unnamed pioneer, was discovered in the early 1900s when the irrigation canal was being dug. The pioneer was a member of the 1845 Lost Meek Party that were left to fend for themselves when Stephen Meek, leader of the wagon train, abandoned the group, leaving the entire party alone in southeastern Oregon. Near the grave, canal builders discovered a fallen juniper, with the words "sacred to the memory of Je__ie." As the name was not completely readable, is not known whether the person was male or female. The current burial site is maintained by the local historical society. The irrigation project workers moved the casket, relocating the grave to its present location, only a few yards from the original burial site. The GPS coordinates for the gravesite are: 44.03.278 N • 121.01.561 W. A broken wagon wheel and cemented rock grave marker honor this pioneer traveler.

Lost Pioneer Grave

Directions to the Lost Pioneer
Grave: *(return to the intersection of Alfalfa and Dodds)*

0.0 miles:
Turn left on Dodds Road, near the Alfalfa community sign.

1.6 miles:
Come to an unmarked road. Turn left onto this dirt BLM road, passing through a green gate.

2.0 miles:
A fork in the road. Stay right.

2.6 miles:
Veer left and stay parallel to the canal.

3.7 miles:
A wagon wheel, the grave and the historical marker on left.

Wagon train ruts near Alfalfa

Alfalfa to Powell Butte

Distance:
15.7 miles

Directions:
From the Alfalfa School, return west on Alfalfa Market Road.

Points En Route

(mileage from the old Alfalfa School)

0.5 miles:
Turn right onto Johnson Ranch Road. Powell Butte, an ancient cinder cone volcano, is in the distance.

3.6 miles:
Log barn on the right.

4.5 miles:
Entering Crook County.

7.9 miles:
An old cabin sits approximately 0.2 miles on the right.

8.4 miles:
Old farmstead.

8.8 miles:
Stop sign. Keep right, taking Powell Butte Road.

11.6 miles:
Intersection with Shumway Road. Stay left on Powell Butte Road. (Note:The Powell Butte Cemetery is 1.0 mile on Shumway Road.)

13.1 miles:
Old, weathered outbuildings.

13.3 miles:
Interesting rock-lined structure.

14.4 miles:
Intersection of Powell Butte Road and Highway 126. The Powell Butte post office is located here. Turn right onto Highway 126.

15.4 miles:
Powell Butte Community Hall, built in 1916.

15.7 miles:
Powell Butte

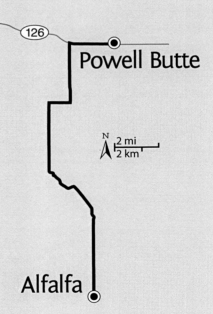

Powell Butte

Elevation: 3,096 feet

Location:
44.14.872 N • 121.01.028 W

Services:
gas, food

The Powells, relatives of circuit rider Joab Powell (who founded the Providence Church in Linn County), were the first settlers in the area. Powell Butte, the name given to the community, is named to honor this family of pioneers and is also the name given to the 5225-foot extinct volcano that towers above the community. Farming is the main economic activity in the area. Non-farming locals commute to nearby Redmond for employment.

Points of Interest

- **Powell Butte School**
  In 1923, this replaced a one-room school.

- **Powell Butte Church**
  Constructed the same year as the school. A newer addition to the growing church was recently completed.

- **Powell Butte Store**
  Old photos on the wall inside the store show Powell Butte as it was in 1928.

Powell Butte School

Powell Butte to Redmond

Distance:
7.3 miles

Directions:
From the Powell Butte Store, go west on Highway 126 toward Redmond. A deep canyon prohibits direct road travel from Powell Butte to O'Neil.

Points En Route

(mileage from the store)

5.9 miles:
National Guard Training Site.

6.0 miles:
Redmond (city limits).

6.7 miles:
Redmond Forest Service Air Center.

7.3 miles:
Downtown Redmond

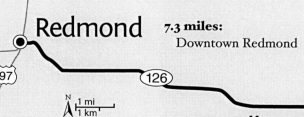

Redmond

Elevation: 3,002 feet

Location:
44.16.432 N • 121.10.227 W

Services:
gas, food, lodging, B&B

Many of the north central communities are around 100 years old, including Redmond, named for Frank and Josephine Redmond, early settlers in what is now one of Oregon's most rapidly growing cities. Like Bend, Redmond is growing exponentially, with recent additions to its school system and infrastructure. The first Redmond post office opened in 1905 and the town was platted in 1906. Aided by the 1911 arrival of the railroad and electricity, along with the development of irrigation canals, Redmond began its steady increase in population to become the second largest city in Central Oregon. Farming, tourism and recreation, services and an abundance of sunshine make the Redmond area a desirable place to live. Redmond has been home to the US Air Force training center since 1943. A major fire destroyed almost three entire blocks of businesses in 1927.

Redmond Hotel

Points of Interest

- **Ehret Brothers Store**
(251 SW 6th)
The oldest standing commercial business building in town, this department store was built in 20 days.

- **Lynch and Roberts Store**
(403 SW 6th)
A general mercantile store built in 1917. The building housed the Redmond Potato Show, precursor to the County Fair.

- **First National Bank**
(404 SW 6th)
From 1919 to 1973, this building was the center of Redmond's Banking.

- **Davidson Meat Market**
(412 SW 6th)
Built in 1921 to look like the First National Bank Building, which stands next door.

- **Irvin Furniture Store**
(421 SW 6th)
The commercial building is constructed of stone mined from Eastern Washington. This 1912 store was a mortuary, coffin making facility and grocery store.

Ehret Brothers Store

Redmond

Points of Interest (continued)

- **Butler Drug Store** (*453 SW 6th*)
  This was the first independent drugstore in town, built in 1915. Its owner died of influenza during the 1918 epidemic.

- **Landaker Building** (*457 SW 6th*)
  Built in 1919, this structure was Redmond's first pool hall. The upper two floors of apartments were added in the 1930s.

- **C.O. Co-operative Creamery** (*640 SW Evergreen*)
  Constructed in 1926, the creamery was updated in the 1940s and closed in the 1960s.

- **Redmond Hotel** (*521 SW 6th*)
  The current structure replaced the 1906 Hotel that burned in 1927. In the late 1920s, the hotel and restaurant owner daily walked into the middle of street and rang a bell, letting business owners know that it was lunchtime.

- **Atkinson Building** (*535 SW 6th*)
  Once the home of a movie theater and hotel, this building was constructed in 1922.

- **Presbyterian Church** (*641 SW Cascade*)
  Opened in 1912 and remodeled in both 1944 and 1948, the church is the oldest in Redmond.

- **Cunning House** (*215 SW 7th*)
  The 1918 home of Max Cunning, successful lawyer and one of Redmond's first city recorders.

- **Irvin House** (*417 7th*)
  Irvin built his 1912 furniture store and house in the same year. He eventually gave up his furniture business to become the local mortician.

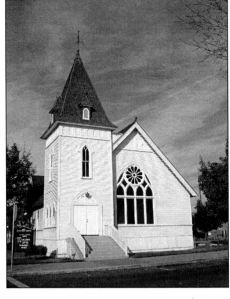

Presbyterian Church

- **Roberts House** (*111 NW 8th*)
  While not the first owner of this 1913 home, Roberts owned and operated a general merchandise store for over 50 years.

- **Methodist Church** (*122 NW 10th*)
  This second-oldest church in town was built in 1912 at the corner of Forest and 8th, and was moved to its current location in 1983.

- **Dr. Hosch House** (*511 SW 12th*)
  This 1911 Craftsman-style house, that once had its own tennis court, is one of the oldest remaining houses in town.

- **Dobson House** (*1408 Evergreen Ave*)
  Another Craftsman, this 1914 bungalow was home to Guy Dobson, founder of Redmond's Bank of Commerce in 1910.

Lynch and Roberts Store

Redmond to O'Neil

Distance:
  8.9 miles

Directions:
  From the intersection of Highway 97 and East Antler, travel west on East Antler.

Points En Route

(mileage from the intersection of East Antler and Highway 97)

0.2 miles:
  Crossing an irrigation canal and then railroad tracks.

0.7 miles:
  At the stop sign, turn left onto NE 9th Street.

1.2 miles:
  Continue on NE 9th, crossing Hemlock Avenue.

1.7 miles:
  Stop sign. Turn right onto NE Negus Way.

2.1 miles:
  Golf course.

3.4 miles:
  Weathered barn and old outbuildings.

3.6 miles:
  Intersection with Yucca. Turn left. Note the basalt fence on the left.

4.3 miles:
  Turn right on O'Neil Highway. At this intersection is the Crooked River Railroad Company, a dinner train complete with a murder mystery dramatic production, wild-west train robbery and scenic views of the Crooked River.

4.8 miles:
  At the power station, keep right, following the O'Neil Highway.

5.1 miles:
  Buena Vista Cattle Ranch. Look for old barns and outbuildings.

5.4 miles:
  Crossing railroad tracks. Note intermittent basalt rock fencing created as farmers cleared their land.

6.4 miles:
  Redmond Tallow Company.

7.8 miles:
  Old cabin on the left.

8.2 miles:
  Begin the descent to the valley floor.

8.8 miles:
  Sand and Gravel Company.

8.9 miles:
  O'Neil

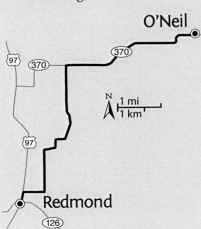

O'Neil

Elevation: 2,825 feet

Location:
44.19.827 N • 121.05.255 W

Services:
none

Immigrant William O'Neil began raising sheep and farming in 1881, lending his name to this small community. First settled in 1873 by the Carmical family, O'Neil once boasted a general store and school. Farming and ranching keep local residents busy. O'Neil was once a major railroad stop for transporting wool and mutton. The depot and station no longer exist.

Points of Interest

- **The O'Neil Farmhouse**
  The farm and home date to the 1880s.

O'Neil Stage Stop

Outbuilding

O'Neil to Lone Pine

Distance:
4.1 miles

Directions:
From the O'Neil farmhouse, proceed north and go left on Lone Pine Road.

Points En Route

(mileage from the old O'Neil farmhouse)

0.2 miles:
Railroad crossing, site of a station and large warehouse.

0.5 miles:
The former stage stop, now a private residence. A unique tower stands adjacent to this old home.

1.2 miles:
Intersection with Smith Rock Way. Continue right on North Lone Pine Road.

2.3 miles:
Old grain elevator.

4.1 miles:
Lone Pine

Lone Pine

Elevation: 2,875 feet

Location:
44.22.680 N • 121.04.087 W

Services:
none

Long since removed, a lone pine tree once stood near the crossroads of Lone Pine Road and Lone Pine Lane. Other than the school and a few farms, not much remains of this farming and ranching community. The railroad bypassed the town, first settled in the 1890s, impeding its growth. Lone Pine is home to the Walking H Ranch, where Clydesdale horses are raised and trained.

Points of Interest

- **Lone Pine Schools**
  The 1951 building sits in front of the old one- room schoolhouse built in the 1920s. A wagon and wishing well adorn the former school grounds that are now private property.

Lone Pine Road

abandoned building in Lone Pine

Lone Pine to Terrebonne

Distance:
   10.3 miles

Directions:
   At the intersection of Lone Pine Road and Lone Pine Lane, turn onto Lone Pine Lane.

Points En Route

(mileage from the intersection of Lone Pine Road and Lone Pine Lane, turn onto Lone Pine Lane)

0.1 miles:
   Abandoned farmhouse.

0.2 miles:
   Another abandoned property.

0.3 miles:
   And another.

0.7 miles:
   Newer log home.

1.0 miles:
   NW Lone Pine Lane becomes N Lone Pine Lane.

2.0 miles:
   Turn left onto NW Butler Road.

2.2 miles:
   Old, derelict home. Note the bottles hung on the barbed wire fencing.

2.9 miles:
   Turn right onto Lone Pine Road.

4.8 miles:
   Turn right onto NW Smith Rock Way.

6.2 miles:
   Crossing the irrigation canal.

8.1 miles:
   Intersection with NW 17th. Turn right onto Smith Rock Way. The entrance to the 1919 Terrebone Cemetery is 100 yards past the intersection.

8.4 miles:
   Willow Creek Ranch.

8.6 miles:
   Turn left toward Terrebonne. For a side trip, turn right onto Wilcox Avenue to visit Smith Rock State Park.

10.1 miles:
   Turn right onto NE Smith Rock Way.

10.3 miles:
   Terrebonne

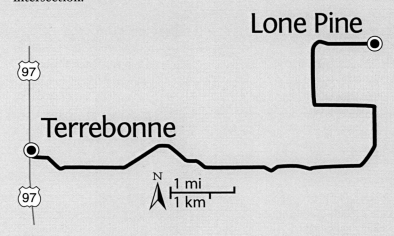

Smith Rock

Terrebonne

Elevation: 2,833 feet

Location:
44.21.060 N • 121.10.389 W

Services:
gas, food

This community was first called Hillman but when the post office opened in 1911, the name changed to Terrebonne from the French *terra* (earth) and *bonne* (good); hence, "good earth." The Central Oregon Pumpkin Company, one of the state's largest producers of pumpkins, is located here.

Ladies Pioneer Club

Points of Interest

- **Old Train Depot and Warehouse**
  (8286 Smith Rock Way)
  Moved to its current location from across the street, the old depot is undergoing complete remodeling and will become the Old Depot Restaurant.

- **Terrebonne Grange**
  (11th and Smith Rock Way)
  Terrebonne Grange number 663 was built in 1924.

- **Ladies Pioneer Club** *(8330 11th)*
  Older than the grange, this building was constructed in 1912.

- **Smith Rock Community Church** *(11th and C)*
  The oldest remaining church in Terrebonne, constructed in the 1920s.

- **Ferguson Market**
  (11th and Highway 97)
  The original storefront faced 11th Street, which was the main road through town.

- **Smith Rock State Park**
  (travel 4.7 miles on Smith Rock Way)
  Picnic, camp, hike, bird watch and rock climb. Hikers can take a relatively easy walk around Smith Rock or hike up steps and follow the path to its crest, which affords breathtaking views.

Terrebonne Grange

Terrebonne to Culver

Distance:
16.6 miles

Directions:
Go north on 11th Avenue, past the grange and Ladies Pioneer Club.

Points En Route

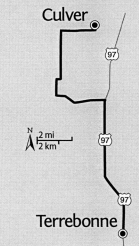

Culver

Terrebonne

(mileage from 11th and Smith Rock Way)

0.5 miles:
Turn right on Highway 97, proceeding toward Madras and Portland.

2.9 miles:
Peter Skene Ogden Viewpoint access road. The viewpoint offers marvelous views of the Crooked River Gorge. Ogden, who scouted this area in the 1820s, was the first explorer to see its sheer basalt cliffs. Watch for river otters in the Crooked River below.

3.1 miles:
Crossing the dramatic Crooked River.

6.0 miles:
Opal Lane. The site of the former community of Opal that derived its name from the voluminous spring near the Crooked River (the water source for nearby Culver and Metolius). The foundation of the 1911 Opal City School House is visible along the dirt road to the left.

8.0 miles:
Turn left onto Monroe Lane. Junipers dominate the landscape.

10.5 miles:
Crossing an irrigation canal.

10.6 miles:
Railroad track crossing and change in flora.

10.9 miles:
Veer right onto SW Green Drive.

11.9 miles:
Turn right onto LaSalle Lane.

12.1 miles:
Turn left onto SW Green Drive.

14.9 miles:
Turn right onto SW Iris Lane, near the power substation.

15.9 miles:
At the stop sign, turn left on Cove Palisades.

16.0 miles:
Turn right onto SW Iris lane.

16.2 miles:
Crossing railroad tracks.

16.6 miles:
Culver

Culver

Elevation: 2,626 feet

Location:
44.31.492 N • 121.12.610 W

Services:
gas, food

Culver, idyllically located between Juniper and Round Buttes, was first settled in the late 1800s, and named to honor O. G. Collver. The post office opened in 1900 and Culver was briefly the county seat from 1914 to 1916. The seat of government shifted, as local residents tell, when marauding Madras residents entered the Culver City Hall, absconded the county records and transferred power to their city. Culver is an agricultural community, thanks to water from the irrigation canals. Major crops include potatoes, garlic, grasses, grains and mint.

Points of Interest

- **Culver Courthouse**
  (1st and E Street)
  The building, now housing the Culver Store and gift shop, was built as the Jefferson County Courthouse.

- **Culver Grange** *(SW Iris Lane and SW Culver Highway)*
  Grange number 227 sits alone on the outskirts of town.

- **Culver City Park** *(on D Street)*
  Restrooms, playground, ball fields and picnic areas.

- **Culver City Hall**
  (Culver Highway and A Street)
  Displayed in the building's council chambers is the 1914 "Culver County Seat" sign, a reminder of Culver as a former throne of power.

Culver to Metolius

Distance:
4.2 miles

Directions:
From the Culver Fire Department and City Hall on Culver Highway, travel north toward Metolius. Note the wonderful views of the snow-covered mountain peaks of the Cascade Range in the distance. Mountain names are, in order from south to north, Bachelor, Broken Top, South Sister, Middle Sister, North Sister, Trout Creek Butte, Black Crater, Black Butte, Washington, Three Fingered Jack, Jefferson, Ollalie Butte and Hood.

Points En Route

(mileage from the Culver Fire Department)

0.2 miles:
Unique Quonset hut structure.

2.7 miles:
Intersection with Franklin Lane; go straight. Left, 0.6 miles, is the 1910 German Cemetery.

4.2 miles:
Metolius

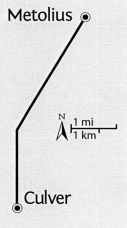

Metolius

Elevation: 2,515 feet

Location:
44.35.213 N • 121.10.713 W

Services:
gas, food, B&B, RV Park

Metolius Train Depot

Metolius began as a German settlement in the 1880s. City records contain minutes of early city meetings that are handwritten in German. The community gets its name from the Metolius River, which begins as a gushing spring near Camp Sherman. The origin of the word is not known, but many think it means "salmon water." The coming of a railroad spur in 1905 was a boon to the town. By 1911, a post office, roundhouse, and train depot were constructed. The town incorporated in 1913, but water was a serious problem for this small, growing community. Like Culver, it gets its water supply from Opal Springs. The first church in Northern Crook County was built in Metolius, although it no longer stands.

Points of Interest

- **Metolius Train Depot**
  (6th and Washington)
  Constructed in 1911, the round house was removed in the 1930s when the main rail line was moved to Bend. The spur line was called the Oregon Trunk Line. An old signal is on display in back of the depot and the Burlington-Northern Railroad Company now uses the rails.

- **Sweet Virginia's Bed and Breakfast** *(407 6th)*
  This 1915 home features leaded glass windows.

- **City Park**
  (on Wilson between 6th and 7th)
  Playground, picnic, restrooms and a covered area.

- **Old House** *(8th and Adams)*
  Beautiful early Metolius home.

- **Metolius Park** *(Butte and Hood)*
  A triangle-shaped park with picnic area, restrooms and playground.

- **Site of Metolius Hotel**
  (7th and Culver Highway)
  The 1917 hotel burned to the ground in 1971. Photos of the structure and the fire are displayed in the city hall.

Metolius to Madras

Distance:
2.3 miles

Directions:
From the north city limits at the intersection of SW Dover and the Culver Highway, proceed north toward Madras.

Points En Route

(mileage from the intersection of SW Dover and Culver Highway)

0.7 miles:
An old barn on the left.

2.3 miles:
Fairgrounds and RV Park.

2.3 miles:
Madras

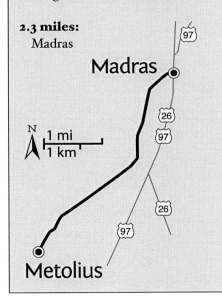

Madras

Elevation: 2,257 feet

Location:
44.38.014 N • 121.07.712 W

Services:
gas, food, lodging, B&B, RV parks

Madras, the Jefferson County seat of government since 1916, is situated in a large basin. The post office opened in 1903 and the town incorporated in 1911, owing initial growth and development to the railroad that came through town the same year. Madras has experienced resurgences in growth after the Great Depression and again in the last ten years. Recreation, farming, and the service industry aid its rapid development.

Madras Hotel

Points of Interest

- **Jefferson County Museum** *(34 SE D)*
  Housed in the 1917 city hall, the museum has interesting displays about area history, including its Native American heritage.

- **IOOF Hall** *(5th and D)*
  Built in 1917 with a saloon downstairs and lodge upstairs.

- **Old Jail** *(6th and D)*
  Built in 1918, the jail stands behind the courthouse.

- **Madras Hotel** *(171 C)*
  The old hotel, with beautiful leaded glass windows, opened in 1911 and is now a real estate office.

- **Sahalee Park** *(7th and C)*
  Picnic area, restrooms, and playground.

- **Freedom Christian Fellowship Church** *(8th and D)*
  One of Madras' oldest churches.

- **Jefferson County Library** *(8th and E)*
  The library, once a church, has been remodeled to hold the county's collection of books and periodicals.

- **Jackson House** *(5th and E)*
  The oldest remaining house in town, built in 1902.

- **Old Downtown Businesses** *(5th Street between C and D)*
  The town's 1905 businesses housed in this street's buildings were – from C toward D – a bakery, goldsmith shop, art gallery, bookstore, mercantile store, photography salon, and an IOOF building with saloon.

Madras to Paxton

Distance:
  6.1 miles

Directions:
  From the Junction of Highways 97 and 26, proceed north on Highway 97.

Points En Route

(mileage from the Intersection of Highways 97 and 26)

1.0 miles:
  Two old gas pumps, from an old service station.

2.6 miles:
  Turn left onto Cora Drive.

3.5 miles:
  Cora Drive becomes Clark Drive.

5.4 miles:
  Piles of rock, left by farmers clearing their land to make the soil tillable.

5.9 miles:
  Turn left onto NE Fir Lane.

6.1 miles:
  Paxton (site)

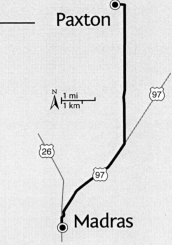
Paxton
Madras

Paxton

Elevation: 2,202 feet

Location:
44.42.712 N • 121.05.855 W

Services:
none

Paxton, one of twenty-four towns and communities in the United States with that name, was a rail stop named for G.L. Paxton, a local landowner and farmer. A train depot and warehouse once stood near the tracks, but the community never had a post office. When the train ceased stopping at Paxton in the 1930s, the abandoned depot and warehouse were removed.

Points of Interest

- **Remains of Paxton Farm**
  (near the corner of Clark and Fir)
  The last outbuildings from the Paxton homestead stand in the field near this intersection.

Remains of Paxton Farm

Paxton railroad tracks

Paxton to Gateway

Distance:
5.3 miles

Directions:
From the railroad tracks, return to the intersection of Clark Drive and Fir Road.

Points En Route

(mileage from the railroad tracks)

0.2 miles:
Intersection of Clark Road and Fir Road. Turn left onto Clark Road.

1.1 miles:
At the "Y," veer left, staying on Clark Drive.

1.2 miles:
6285 NE Clark Drive. Abandoned homestead with outbuildings.

3.2 miles:
Clark Drive becomes NE Buckley Lane.

3.6 miles:
Begin descent into the valley; spectacular views of Gateway on the valley floor.

4.8 miles:
Gateway Missionary Baptist Church.

4.9 miles:
"Tongue in cheek" Gateway City Hall and Morgue.

5.2 miles:
Pumphouse Park. Picnic and play.

5.3 miles:
Gateway

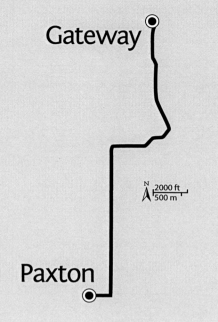

Gateway

Elevation: 1,817 feet
Location:
44.46.564 N • 121.05.024 W
Services:
none

Gateway is aptly named as it sits in a small valley carved by Trout Creek, which runs through the small community. The post office opened in 1913 and the town never incorporated.

Points of Interest

- **Gateway Train Depot**
  (Clemens Drive and Market Street)
  Once a busy depot, the train no longer stops in this small burg. The depot was built circa 1913.

- **Noah Vibbert General Store**
  (Market Street)
  For many years after opening in 1914, this abandoned, false-fronted building was alive with activity.

- **Road to Trout Creek Recreational Site**
  (3.3 miles north on Clemens Drive)
  This gravel road leads to excellent fishing and camping.

Noah Vibbert General Store

Gateway Train Depot

Gateway to Willowdale

Distance:
13.6 miles

Directions:
From the depot at Gateway, backtrack 0.2 miles south on Clark Drive to NE McFarland Lane.

Points En Route

(mileage from the depot)

0.2 miles:
Turn left onto NE McFarland Lane.

0.4 miles:
Pavement ends.

0.7 miles:
Bee hives.

1.7 miles:
McFarland Lane bears right and becomes NE Rex Drive.

1.9 miles:
NE Rex Drive turns left, becoming NE Eagle Lane.

2.0 miles:
Sagebrush Spring, a former small spring that brought respite to early settlers and their livestock.

2.1 miles:
Intersection with Emerson Drive. Turn right.

3.0 miles:
Basalt rock wall, stacked by farmers clearing their fields.

3.4 miles:
Turn left onto NE Quaale Drive. Pavement returns.

6.3 miles:
Intersection with Old Highway 97. Turn right, travel north toward Willowdale.

9.2 miles:
To the right is one of Richardson's thunder egg shops and agate beds.

9.2 miles:
Narrow bridge.

10.6 miles:
Striking red rock outcropping.

11.0 miles:
Intersection of Old Highway 97 and Highway 97. Turn left toward Willowdale. This point is called Lyle Gap, named for the 1877 settler that homesteaded near this point.

11.5 miles:
The road to Ashwood. For a beautiful, paved side trip, turn right and travel the seventeen miles to Ashwood. The route offers beautiful views of the valley below as the road winds to the top of a canyon. The summit, approximately 13 miles from Lyle Gap, is called Pony Butte, with an elevation of 3251 feet. Located on Trout Creek, Ashwood was settled by miners in the 1870s and its post office opened in 1898. The name "Ashwood" is derived from the joining of Ash Butte, from the Oregon King Mine, and Whitfield Wood, early miner and settler. A few homes, the 1899 store that has been remodeled into a home, the 1902 Ashwood Community Church, the Ashwood Grange #802, the 1898 Ashwood School, and the 1898 Ashwood post office, which remains open, are visages of Ashwood's busier and more robust days. Once gold was discovered in the quartz rock near the creek, saloons, hotels, livery stables and mercantile stores opened for business. The

Canyon near Ashwood

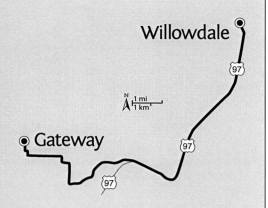

Oregon King Mine, the major producer, was about three miles north and west of the current community. The Red Jacket Mine and other smaller claims never produced much gold ore, and quickly closed. The Oregon King continued to operate for several years, but closed when lesser quantities of gold were found in the quartz. Talk of a stamp mill died, as did the miners' hopes for riches, when the gold-filled vein thinned to nothing. Small amounts of silver and mercury were also mined. Although little gold was discovered here, many fossils can be found in the area. The side trip to Ashwood is worth the time and effort.

13.6 miles:
Willowdale

Willowdale

Elevation: 1,771 feet

Location:
44.48.371 N • 120.56.004 W

Services:
none

The actual site of Willowdale rests several hundred yards south of the bridge that spans Trout Creek. Willowdale was an important stage stop on The Dalles to California stage line. Unfortunately, the old stage stop, post office, and livery stable burned to the ground in the 1940s. A restaurant that burned in the 1980s replaced the stage stop at the same location. The

Hay Crew Cookhouse

exact locality of the stage stop is the wide spot in the road on the left at 13.6 miles. A few homes to the north of the stage stop make up what remains of the community. Willowdale is located in the bottomlands where Pony Creek and Hay Creek join. A tree-lined entrance to one of the more successful Willowdale farms lies a short distance to the north. The Willowdale post office opened in 1928, only to close in 1937. Willowdale is named for the willows that grow abundantly near the creek beds. According to *Ripley's Believe it or Not* "strange, but true" category, a unique law was passed by the Willowdale community, making it illegal for a man to curse while being amorous with his wife. Cattle ranching, sheep farming and hay growing are common in this valley recess, with the R-2 Ranch owning much of the property on both sides of the highway. Highway 197 splits with Highway 97 to the north at 0.6 miles. Highway 197 leads to Shaniko and Highway 97 heads to Antelope.

house in Ashwood

road near Willowdale

62

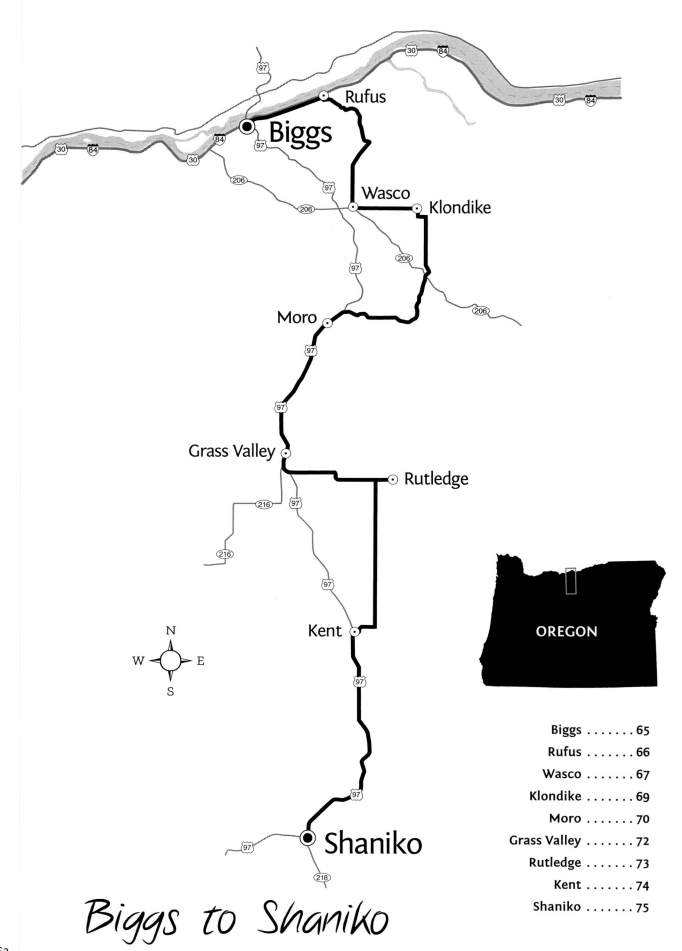

Rufus

Biggs

Wasco

Klondike

Moro

Grass Valley

Rutledge

Kent

OREGON

Shaniko

Biggs to Shaniko

Wind Generators and Ghost Towns in the Grasslands

Biggs to Shaniko (81 miles)

This route begins at Biggs, a transportation hub located on the Columbia River, which has changed dramatically since it was tamed by a series of dams that connect the Oregon and Washington riverbanks near here. Construction of The Dalles Dam and the John Day Dam, which are less than 30 miles apart, have made the mid-Columbia region an important irrigation source and recreation center.

Even though most wagon train traffic ended with the coming of the Transcontinental Railroad in 1869, some settlers continued to travel to Oregon by wagon until the early 1900s. Today wheat is the dominant crop in this area, where wind generators stand tall in the middle of miles of grain fields, turning constantly in the wind.

wind turbines near Klondike

Biggs

Elevation: 236 feet

Location:
45.40.139 N • 120.50.065 W

Services:
gas, food, lodging

Biggs, once known as Spanish Hollow due to its location at the mouth of a canyon, is named for 1880s pioneer W.H. Biggs. When the railroad to The Dalles came through Biggs in 1884, a rail station and post office were constructed. While relatively few people live here, Biggs is a key juncture and shipping terminus on the Columbia, located at the busy intersection of Highway 97 and Interstate 84. Wheat fields on the plateau and fruit orchards near the river form the economic mainstays of this small community. Before the high cost of electricity used in processing metal forced the Alcoa Aluminum mill to shut down, many mill workers made Biggs their home. Biggs Picture Jasper can be found in many locations near town, especially near the river in Spanish Hollow. Biggs was the last important pioneer stop before the end of the Oregon Trail in The Dalles.

bridge over the Columbia River in Biggs

Points of Interest

- **Mid-Columbia Barge Elevator** (*91589 Barge Way*)
  Huge barges, full of wheat, are loaded and unloaded near this large elevator.

- **Mid-Columbia Railroad Elevator** (*91385 Railroad Lane*)
  A shipping center for many regional farmers who bring their crops to Biggs for railroad transport.

- **Stonehenge Replica** (*cross the Columbia, taking Highway 97 north for 3.2 miles; turn right at intersection of Washington State Highway 14*)
  An exact replica of the Druid ruins of English fame, this concrete structure honors WWI Veterans.

- **Maryhill Castle Museum** (*at the intersection of Highway 97 and Washington Highway 14, turn left on Highway 14 and travel 4.5 miles to the Museum*)
  In 1914, Sam Hill – railroad executive, highway engineer, and entrepreneur – began construction of this mansion on Maryhill (named for both his daughter and his wife), a 6,000-acre tract standing 800 feet above the river. Hill passed away in 1931, and nine years later this three-story brick and concrete structure opened to the public as a museum. A pedestal-sized statue, Rodin's *"The Thinker,"* is permanently displayed at the gallery along with an extensive collection of Native American artifacts and regalia.

building in Biggs

Biggs to Rufus

Distance:
5.0 miles

Directions:
At the intersection of Highway 97 and Biggs-Rufus Highway, turn left, traveling east on Frontage Road.

Points En Route

(mileage from the intersection of Biggs-Rufus Highway and Main Street)

0.1 miles:
Bridge, spanning Spanish Hollow.

1.3 miles:
View of Stonehenge (to the left across the river).

5.0 miles:
Rufus (intersection of Biggs-Rufus Highway and Main Street)

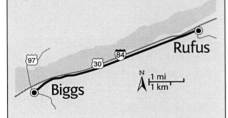

Rufus

Elevation: 235 feet

Location:
45.41.713 N • 120.44.140 W

Services:
gas, food, lodging, RV Park

The relocated community of Rufus was named for 1884 Scottish settler Rufus Wallis, who later moved to the Washington side of the river in order to better run his ferry business that crossed the Columbia at this point. The community was incorporated in 1965, after relocating to its present site following the construction of The Dalles Dam and the formation of Lake Celilo. It is new, by Oregon standards. There is an odd configuration of streets due to the retooling of the town center. Tourism, recreation, wheat and fruit farming make up the local economy. The old highway, constructed in 1927, gave life to the small community, which declined upon closure of the Alcoa Aluminum Plant and completion of Interstate 84 in the late 1960s. During WWII, in an area of the town now buried under reservoir water, the army built pontoon boats and bridges for use in the European Theater.

Rufus School

Points of Interest

- **Rufus School** *(304 2nd Street)*
Erected in 1926, the venerable building is now the community center.

- **Rufus Grange #826**
(Main and 3rd)
Built in 1927, the same year as the old highway.

- **Rufus City Hall** *(4th and Main)*
High enough to have survived the creation of Lake Celilo, the City Hall is almost eighty years old.

- **D.J. and H. Rock Museum**
(1/2 mile west on old Highway 30)
Owned by Howard Dolph, a collector of rocks and gems for eighty years. Howard has a large collection of thunder eggs, petrified wood, agates and Biggs Picture Jasper.

- **Giles French Park**
(south of John Day Dam)
Restrooms, picnicking, camping, windsurfing and fishing.

- **John Day Dam** *(go east to exit 109)*
The dam, which took 10 years to construct, opened in 1968. The visitors' center closed following the collapse of the twin towers on 9/11.

Grain Elevator near Rufus

road between Rufus and Wasco

Rufus to Wasco

Distance:
9.2 miles

Directions:
From Main Street and the Biggs–Rufus Highway, go south on Canyon Road.

Points En Route

(mileage from Main and Canyon)

3.0 miles:
Old farmstead on the right. Acres of wheat and rolling hills with Mt. Hood in the distance.

9.2 miles:
Wasco

(map showing route from Rufus to Wasco with highways 84, 97, and 206, N scale 2 mi / 2 km)

Crossfield's General Merchandise Store

Wasco

Elevation: 1,298 feet

Location:
45.35.556 N • 120.41.835 W

Services:
gas, food, lodging

Wasco, named for Native Americans who were part of the great Chinook Nation, was first settled in 1870 and incorporated in 1898. Wasco County, once the largest county in the United States (spanning more than five states), is still larger than Rhode Island and boasts the largest percentage of cultivated land in Oregon. Wheat, barley and cattle compose the economy of this community.

Points of Interest

- **Wasco School** *(903 Barnett)*
  Opened in 1916.

- **Oskaloosa Hotel**
  (Clark and Barnett)
  The 1903 hotel is now an antique store.

- **Crossfield's General Merchandise Store**
  (Clark and Armsworthy)
  Making its grand opening in 1898, the store sold a little of everything.

- **Crossfield Mansion** *(620 Davis)*
  At one time, this beautifully restored home served as the community hospital, though it is once again a private residence.

- **Railroad Depot**
  (Clark and Fullerton)
  The 104 year-old Columbia Southern Line Depot, located in the center of town, is surrounded by a park. The great flood of 1964 took out the rail line.

- **City Hall** (*1017 Clark*)
  This 1903 center of civic commerce houses the city library.

- **Wasco Market** (*Clark Street*)
  Wild meat dressing and cutting services are available as well as the usual grocery items.

- **Wasco Bank** (*1209 Clark*)
  Held the accounts of wheat, barley and cattle farmers.

- **Hotel Sherman and Goose Pit Tavern** (*1210 Clark*)
  The hotel burned in 1956 and only the first floor was re-built. The original hotel garage for guest's autos still stands one block from the renovated building. Photos on the wall of the rebuilt restaurant and bar show the building as it was before the fire.

- **Wasco United Methodist Church** (*910 Wilson*)
  The church was built in 1902.

- **Wasco Drug and Variety** (*1016 Clark*)
  Chinese laborers helped erect the brick building with its unique rock foundation. Note the interior tin roof ceiling that was shipped from San Francisco by rail, then unloaded and carried one block from the depot to this location. The cabinets, all second hand, were installed in 1902 when the building was constructed.

- **City Park** (*Armsworthy and Wilson*)
  Located in the center of town, the park was built around the old railroad depot and is complete with restrooms, caboose and playground equipment.

- **Wasco Methodist Cemetery** (*2 miles north of town off highway 97*)
  Dates to the late 1800s.

Crossfield Mansion

Wasco to Klondike

Distance:
4.5 miles

Directions:
From the corner of Clark and Armsworthy, proceed east on Armsworthy toward Klondike.

Points En Route

(mileage from the intersection of Clark and Armsworthy)

0.3 miles:
Wasco State Airport.

3.4 miles:
Old brick farmhouse.

4.0 miles:
Turn right onto North Klondike Road. Note rows of windmills.

4.5 miles:
Klondike

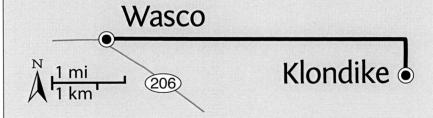

Klondike

Elevation: 1,553 feet

Location:
45.35.056 N • 120.36.808 W

Services:
none

Little remains of Klondike, whose post office opened in 1898 and closed in 1950. Legend says that Klondike's name dates to 1898 when the railroad crew, building a line from Shaniko, deserted their employer to mine for gold in the Klondike region of Alaska. Sadly, the 1907 schoolhouse, a major landmark and community centerpiece, collapsed in 2002. The turbines of the Klondike Wind Farm generate 321 megawatts of electricity and dot the surrounding wheat fields.

Points of Interest

- **Wind Generators:**
  The French-designed generators produce electricity from wind. The generators will turn with wind speeds as low as 5 mph.

- **Grain Elevator:**
  The elevator and farmhouse are all that remain of this small community.

- **Webfoot School:**
  Stands abandoned in a wheat field 4.1 miles east of Klondike, on N. Klondike Road.

Webfoot School

old and new windmills

Klondike to Moro

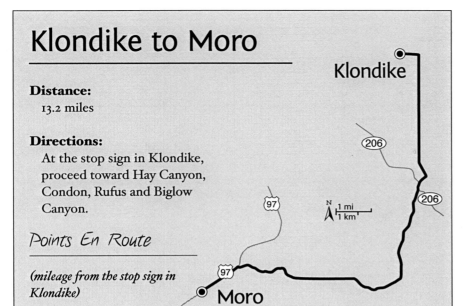

Distance:
13.2 miles

Directions:
At the stop sign in Klondike, proceed toward Hay Canyon, Condon, Rufus and Biglow Canyon.

Points En Route

(mileage from the stop sign in Klondike)

0.5 miles:
PPM Energy substation, where wind is converted to electricity. Turn right onto Sandon Road.

4.3 miles:
Rough road for 0.1 miles.

4.4 miles:
Intersection of Sandon Road and Highway 206. Turn left, traveling south toward Condon on Highway 206.

4.5 miles:
Veer right onto Hay Canyon Road toward Hay Canyon and Harmony.

5.8 miles:
Interesting rock sculpture.

7.2 miles:
Monkland Lane. Turn right toward Monkland and Moro.

7.9 miles:
Monkland, a community named by settlers hailing from a small town of the same name in Ontario, Canada. Monkland is located at the intersection of Lavender Lane and Monkland Lane. The Charles Thompson Homestead, an 1891 Century Farm, still stands. Thompson served as Monkland's first postmaster in 1886.

9.6 miles:
Views of Mt. Hood, Mt. Adams and Mt. Rainier.

11.0 miles:
At the intersection with Heinrich Road, veer left, continuing west on Monkland Lane.

12.2. miles:
Intersection of Monkland Lane and Highway 97; turn left, traveling south on Highway 97.

12.5 miles:
A llama ranch.

12.8 miles:
Century Farm.

13.2 miles:
Moro

Moro

Elevation: 1,794 feet

Location:
45.29.057 N • 120.43.812 W

Services:
gas, food, lodging

Moro, settled in 1868 and incorporated in 1899, serves as the Sherman County seat. It was named for another community in Illinois. The Barnum family, original settlers, built the first store and the first home in the community. In 1918, ten successful farmers joined forces to build a 25,000 square foot hotel, said to be the first hotel west of the Mississippi with private baths and private toilets. The old hotel operated successfully until 1983. It now serves as an antique store, whose owner is trying to restore the building to its former glory. The great flood of 1964 wiped out the Columbia Southern Railroad. Moro is the smallest county seat in Oregon, with a population of approximately 335 people. Wheat farming is the mainstay of this rural community.

Points of Interest

- **Moro Museum**
  (200 Dewey Street)
  Contains much information about early Moro and Wasco County. The 15,000 square foot museum is open May to October and by appointment.

- **City Park** *(next to museum)*
  Restrooms, playground and picnic area near the creek.

- **Presbyterian Church**
  (4th and McCoy)
  Built in 1887, it still holds weekly services.

Moro

Points of Interest (continued)

- **Sherman County Courthouse** (*4th and Court*)
Constructed in 1899 on a hill overlooking town, the magnificent brick structure was recently remodeled.

- **Ornate Victorian Home** (*Birdwell and Main*)
One of Moro's older and more elegant homes.

- **Moro Cemetery** (*go north and west on Van Gilder*)
Gravesites date to the 1880s.

- **Sherman County Fairgrounds** (*East on 1st*)
The annual fair is held in August.

- **Moro Hotel** (*Main and 1st*)
The 25,000 square foot hotel was once the centerpiece of this small community.

- **Victorian Home** (*103 Scott*)
Much gingerbread adorns this old-timer.

- **Moro School** (*Lincoln and Birdwell*)
Continuously in use since its construction in 1917.

Sherman County Courthouse

Moro to Grass Valley

Distance:
9.0 miles

Directions:
From 2nd and Main, take Highway 97 south.

Points En Route

(mileage from the intersection of 2nd and Main)

2.3 miles:
1882 home of the Moore's, prominent early settlers.

2.9 miles:
Victorian homestead.

6.5 miles:
Old farm's root cellar.

7.9 miles:
Intersection with Cemetery Road and the location of the 1890 Grass Valley IOOF Cemetery.

9.0 miles:
Grass Valley

Grass Valley

Elevation: 2,218 feet

Location:
45.21.709 N • 120.47.033 W

Services:
gas, food, lodging, RV Park

Settled in the 1890s and incorporated in 1900, Grass Valley received its name from the naturally growing ryegrass that pioneers stated stood taller than a horse and rider. Grass Valley farmers grow wheat and rye; some grow fruit or raise cattle.

Methodist Church

Points of Interest

- **Grass Valley Baptist Church** *(122 S. Mill St)*
  Three services are held every Sunday in this church that opened in 1894.

- **Grass Valley Mercantile Building** *(Market Street)*
  The old mercantile store was built in the 1890s, and has had multiple uses since then.

- **Grass Valley Store** *(302 North 3rd)*
  Since 1905, this has been the local grocery store.

- **Old House** *(Church and Main)*
  Moved, on rollers, to its present location.

- **Grass Valley School** *(300 block of 4th Street)*
  An old-timer, erected in 1901.

- **Oldest House in Grass Valley** *(620 SW 4th)*
  Needs some work, but is the oldest standing house in town.

- **IOOF Building** *(2nd and Market)*
  This 1941 building replaced the 1898 hall that burned to the ground.

- **Old Tractors and Trucks** *(Railroad and Market)*
  Rows of old tractors and trucks are displayed in a field.

- **Old Home** *(102 4th)*
  Almost as old as the home at Church and Main.

- **Grass Valley RV Park** *(Mill Street)*
  Offers full hook-ups.

- **Victorian Houses** *(407 4th, 502 4th, 510 4th, 610 4th and 1006 4th)*
  Elegant hilltop homes that overlook the community.

- **Methodist Church** *(2nd and Union)*
  A once grand structure that now stands gutted.

Grass Valley to Rutledge

Distance:
6.5 miles

Directions:
From Krusow and Mill (at Highway 97 near the grain elevator) drive south toward Kent.

Points En Route

(mileage from the intersection of Krusow and Mill)

0.7 miles:
Turn left, traveling east onto Rutledge Road.

6.3 miles:
Intersection with Horseshoe Bend Road. Stay on Rutledge.

6.5 miles:
Rutledge

Grass Valley

97

216

N
1 mi
1 km

Rutledge

Rutledge

Elevation: 2,450 feet

Location:
45.20.283 N • 120.38.530 W

Services:
none

The post office opened in 1884 and closed in 1908. Rutledge was named after early settlers who settled here in 1883. Little remains of this small farming community.

Points of Interest

- **Abandoned Rutledge Home**
  This home was located in the center of town. The mercantile store stood across the street from the unattached garage.

- **Rutledge School**
  (*1.2 miles east of the abandoned home – 96341 Rutledge Road*)
  The 1925 school is now a private residence.

Rutledge to Kent

Distance:
10.7 miles

Directions:
From the abandoned Rutledge house, backtrack to Horseshoe Bend Road.

Points En Route

(mileage from the abandoned house)

0.2 miles:
Intersection of Rutledge Road and Horseshoe Bend. Turn left onto Horseshoe Bend.

1.1 miles:
Another windmill, farmhouse, and outbuildings. The crossroads found approximately every mile along this route define the boundaries of homestead land claims.

1.5 miles:
1910 Turpin Hill / Claude Eslinger homesteads down Rosebush Creek, still owned by the family.

4.5 miles:
Bourbon Lane (site of a former

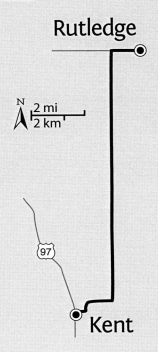

community named for the corn mash that was manufactured near this location).

7.8 miles:
Windmill, the only remains of a farm family's dream.

10.7 miles:
Kent (Horseshoe Bend Road becomes Dobie Road at the Baptist Church)

abandoned home in Rutledge

Kent

Elevation: 2,712 feet

Location:
45.11.613 N • 120.41.356 W

Services:
none

The Kent community was first settled in the 1860s and the post office opened in 1887. The name was allegedly chosen at random, as community members each placed potential names into a hat. Is Kent a living community or a ghost town? Its twenty-three citizens will argue both sides. The school, built in 1937, closed in 1980 and burned shortly thereafter. The gym, whose doors

Kent Grain Elevators

have been removed, is open to the elements, and to locals who gather to play basketball and other games. The old gas station and café was forced to close, as the owners could not afford to upgrade the gas pumps and purify the soil to meet DEQ standards. The old store, however, is scheduled for renovation. A large grain elevator stores crops harvested by local farmers. Locals say that Kent was the setting for Zane Gray's novel *The Desert of Wheat*.

Points of Interest

- **Old Kent Store** (*corner of Highway 97 and Dobie Lane*)
  The old market, with its false front, served the grocery needs of travelers and locals for many years.

- **Kent Diner and Gas** (*highway 97*)
  The station closed when gas was 55 cents a gallon as displayed on a remaining pump.

- **Root Cellar** (*across the street from the old diner*)
  An interesting, stone-covered, metal-lined structure.

- **Old Kent School Gym** (*behind the diner*)
  Basketballs and volleyballs lie on the warped hardwood floors of this gym, open to both the public and the elements.

- **George's Studio** (*Dobie Lane*)
  The art studio and gallery is closed, but still stores artwork belonging to the last owner/operator.

- **Kent Baptist Church** (*Dobie Lane*)
  The church was built and the congregation founded in the 1880s.

- **Mid-Columbia Grain Elevator** (*95185 Dobie Lane*)
  Both modern and old grain elevators sit side by side.

- **False Front Buildings** (*several in a row on Dobie Lane*)
  Intriguing, ghostly appearance.

abandoned store fronts in Kent

Kent to Shaniko

Distance:
15.2 miles

Directions:
From Dobie Point Road and Highway 97, turn left on Highway 97 and travel south.

Points En Route

(mileage from the intersection of Dobie Point Road and Highway 97)

1.5 miles:
Abandoned house, outbuildings and weathervane.

2.7 miles:
1880s Kent Cemetery on the left.

3.5 miles:
Weather vane and root cellar.

4.6 miles:
Wilcox Road. Wilcox is the site of a former community, named for 1880s settlers that lived here.

5.0 miles:
Landscape changes from carefully groomed wheat fields to un-cleared land, erratic rocks, and sagebrush, with occasional grazing cattle.

10.3 miles:
Rise in elevation and appearance of pine trees.

14.9 miles:
Abandoned house of a former Shaniko farmer.

15.2 miles:
Shaniko

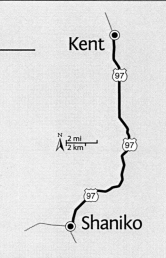

Shaniko

Elevation: 3,341 feet

Location:
45.00.271 N • 120.45.124 W

Services:
gas, food, lodging

First called Cross Hollow in 1879, Shaniko is Oregon's most famous ghost town. The name was changed in 1900, and comes from the Native American pronunciation of "Schnerneckau," the name of an early settler. Shaniko was known as the Inland Wool Capital of the World, with the railroad annually hauling tons of freshly sheared wool to Portland and its textile plants. The community once boasted five saloons, three hotels and numerous other businesses. The creation of synthetics, overgrazing by sheep and several fires eventually reduced Shaniko to its status as a ghost town. The old Shaniko Hotel was the first building to be restored. This restoration lured flocks of tourists to the community and inspired many business owners to restore other structures. No church was ever built in Shaniko as church services were held in the schoolhouse. The church standing in Shaniko today was moved to its current location from another community, yet no Sunday services have ever been held there. A fire in 2005 destroyed many structures, including an old home that, until the fire, served as a bed and breakfast. Since bedrock lies only six inches below the topsoil, there is no cemetery in Shaniko.

Points of Interest

- **Shaniko Hotel** *(4th and E)*
  Constructed in 1901, it now serves as a bed and breakfast.

Shaniko Hotel

- **Cash Store** *(4th and E)*
  Built in 1900 as the Sanford Cash Store, it later became a saloon. This store was the site of Shaniko's first post office.

- **Old City Hall and Jail** *(E Street)*
  Erected in 1901.

- **Water Tower** *(6th and C)*
  One of the earliest and most important structures in the community, the wooden tower was built in 1900.

- **Shaniko School**
  (community center on 3rd)
  Opened in 1901 and now the town's community center.

- **Post Office** *(4th)*
  The new building was erected in 1960. Shaniko's first post office opened in 1879, closed in 1887, and reopened in 1900.

- **Morelli's** *(48812 D Street)*
  Built as a farm home in 1915, this western-style bed and breakfast was open year 'round until it burned to the ground in the summer of 2005.

Shaniko School House

- **Shaniko Church**
  (3rd Street and D)
  Moved from Bakeoven and remodeled in 1962, the structure is actually the old 1899 Bakeoven school. No church services have ever been held here, just weddings, socials and dances. Shaniko never had a church built within city limits.

- **Shaniko Museum** *(4th Street)*
  The 1900 livery stable, once important to sheep and cattle ranchers, is now the museum.

- **Shaniko Sage Museum**
  (behind the old City Hall)
  Displays of historical artifacts and descriptions of Shaniko's past are housed in this newly-constructed building.

- **Sarsaparilla Saloon**
  (behind the city Hall)
  Opened in 1907 as the Moody Garage. The Moody's built and owned the warehouse in town.

- **Newspaper Office**
  (behind the old city hall)
  Newer construction that houses an 1898 printing press.

- **Wool Shipping Barn** *(4th and F Street, near the edge of town)*
  Erected in 1900 at the same time the train came to town. The original barn was 600 feet long, 75% larger than what remains today.

- **Henton House**
  (8 miles south of town)
  The house dates to the 1860s. Gold was discovered in Canyonville and the Henton House became a stage stop, providing wool and mutton to the miners heading to southern Oregon. Henton was the first owner of the Imperial Stock Ranch.

- **Imperial Stock Ranch**
  (the Henton house is part of the Stock Ranch)
  The cattle and sheep ranch dates to the 1870s and still operates today.

Shaniko Jail Wagon

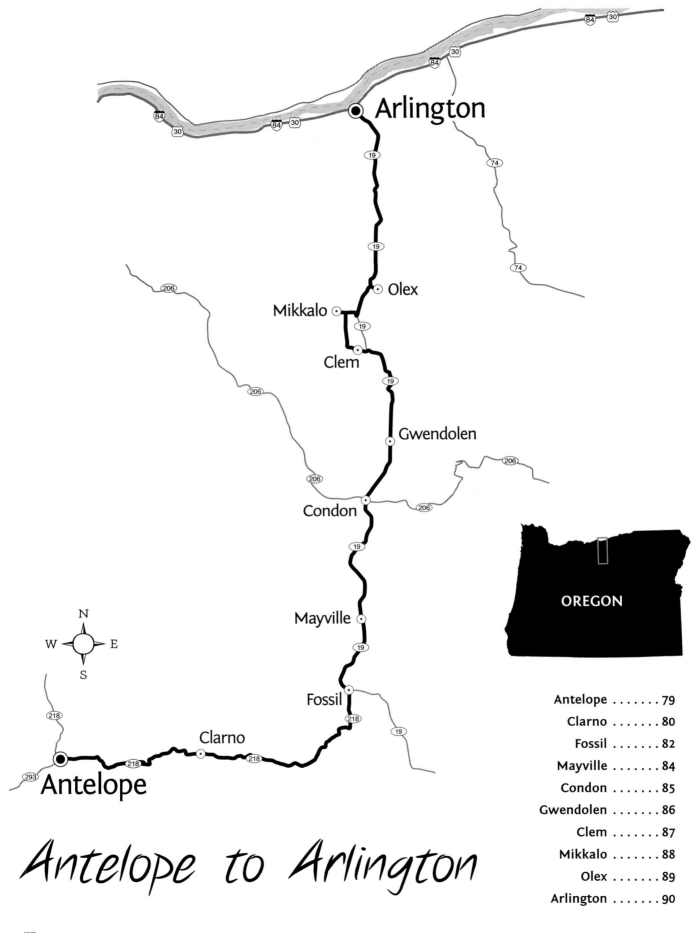

Arlington

Olex

Mikkalo

Clem

Gwendolen

Condon

Mayville

Fossil

Clarno

Antelope

OREGON

Antelope to Arlington

Locating the Meaning of Metasequoia

Antelope to Arlington (83 miles)

This route begins in peaceful, sleepy Antelope – a small, close-knit community besieged by thousands of "Rajneeshees" in the early 1980s, that has since regained its former identity.

From Antelope, the trip continues to Clarno and its brilliantly colored rock formations. The Clarno Unit of the John Day Fossil Beds National Monument has numerous exploration opportunities and provides day-use facilities that await travelers. Take time to dig for fossils behind Wheeler High School, where fossils were discovered when the football field was created.

Make sure to walk around the cemetery in Mayville, looking for the gravesite of Henry Beck and the sad epitaph of his life. Then it's on to Condon, the grade-school home of two Nobel Prize winners, through the back roads and wheat fields of Gwendolen, Mikkalo and Olex, ending in Arlington, a town submerged and then rebuilt in 1968 when the John Day Dam was constructed.

the road near Clarno

Antelope

Elevation: 2,678 feet

Location:
44.54.776 N • 120.43.446 W

Services:
gas, food

The area known as Antelope was probably explored and named by members of Joseph Sherar's group in the 1860s that were hauling supplies to the mines in the John Day area. Sherar is best known for operating a toll bridge across the Deschutes River on the Barlow Cut-off route. Once the bridge was in place, Antelope soon became an important stage stop. The Antelope post office opened in 1871 and was

Antelope Newspaper Office

named for the large numbers of antelope that inhabited the area. Howard Maupin, for whom the community of Maupin is named, served as first postmaster. Maupin was right-hand man to Harry Wheeler (for whom Wheeler County is named) and ran the stagecoach stop. The town flourished until the railroad by-passed the community when it laid tracks to Shaniko instead of Antelope. Despite a major fire that wiped out all but one business in 1898, the community rebuilt and incorporated in 1901. Survival was difficult after the fire and frequent quarrels ended in shootings. The small community struggled to exist until 1981 when the 64,229-acre "Big Muddy" ranch was sold to spiritual leader Bhagwan Shree Rajneesh, who developed a communal society on the property. In a very short time, more than 7,000 neo-sannyasins (followers of the Bhagwan) resided on the ranch. At the time, the population of Antelope proper had dwindled to less than fifty inhabitants. The ever-swelling numbers of Rhajneesh cult members easily overtook the city council and most businesses. Legal and illegal shenanigans by the followers of the Bhagwan and their over-zealous radical efforts to control the area came to an abrupt end in 1985 when Ma Anand Sheela and fifteen of the top commune officials were arrested, sentenced to jail time, and deported. Water problems continue to plague the community, which looks much like it did at the turn of the century. The café, called "The Buddha" when operated by Rajneeshees, is open under a new name. Even though cult members controlling the city council voted to change the town's name to Rajneesh, postal authorities, relying on the efficiency of zip codes, never acknowledged the amended name. Today, only about forty people reside here and the town serves as another example of the continual struggle of small communities to exist.

Points of Interest

- **Antelope Newspaper Office** (*Main*)
  Across the street from the post office, this office dates to 1898. Early Antelope resident and author H.L. Davis, who worked for the paper between 1906 and 1908, wrote the book *Honey in the Horn*. For his journalistic efforts, Davis was presented with the Harper Award in 1935 and the 1936 Pulitzer Prize for his work. Five horseshoes adorn the space above the front door of the old newspaper office.

- **Antelope Post Office** (*Main*)
  One of the postal branches that may be closed due to lack of money.

- **Antelope Shell** (*Main*)
  Closed in the late 1980s.

- **Antelope 76 Station** *(Main)*
  Also closed, and now full of junk.

- **Antelope Police Building and Jail** *(Wallace)*
  Located above and behind the post office, the jail door is in the center of the building. Take caution if you enter the old police station that has no front windows.

- **AOUW Building** *(Main)*
  Built 1898. The Ancient Order of United Workman (AOUW) is an offshoot of the Masons. In 1895, there were more than 300,000 members nationwide. This is thought to be only one of a handful of remaining AOUW Buildings in Oregon.

- **Antelope City Park** *(Main and Union)*
  A small, treed area with picnic tables.

- **Antelope School** *(College and McGreer)*
  The school closed in the 1980s and is under remodel.

- **Tammany Hall** *(Main and Maupin)*
  This run-down building, constructed in 1898 as the civic center, is in need of repair.

- **Antelope Methodist Church** *(College and Union)*
  Now the Community Church, this 1897 structure is the only building that was not lost in the 1898 fire.

- **Old Houses** *(line Main)*
  Most of these homes were constructed between 1898 and 1905. Outhouses stand behind a several of them.

- **Antelope Cemetery** *(off Bennett)*
  Dates to the 1870s.

Clarno

Elevation: 1,319 feet

Location:
44.54.877 N • 120.28.334 W

Services:
none

This ranching community was named for 1866 settler Andrew Clarno, who built a home and barn on the John Day River near Pine Creek. The Clarno post office opened in 1894 and closed in 1949. Clarno was originally located in Gilliam County, but now lies in Wasco County. The first Clarno bridge across the John Day was constructed in 1908. Clarno's chief attraction is the nearby fossil beds in general, and the Clarno Unit Interpretive Area and Fossil Trails in particular. The old grange doubles as the museum and is open sporadically. The schoolhouse was completely restored and is located on private property about one-half mile across the highway from the grange.

Points of Interest

- **Clarno Grange #674**
  (9998 Highway 218)
  The grange doubles as the museum.

- **Clarno House**
  (across from the grange)
  This house, built by Andrew Clarno's son, has been here for more than 100 years.

- **Clarno School**
  (across the highway from the grange)
  The school opened in 1914 and was completely renovated in 2010. It is on private property.

Antelope to Clarno

Distance:
14.9 miles

Directions:
From the intersection of Main and Union (at the Antelope Café), drive east on Main (Highway 218) toward Clarno.

Points En Route

(mileage from the Antelope Café)

0.1 miles:
Keep left on Highway 218. This route follows the state of Oregon's "Journey Through Time Scenic Byway."

6.8 miles:
Summit.

7.5 miles:
Beautiful view to the left.

8.1 miles:
Picturesque ranch and outbuildings.

14.9 miles:
Clarno

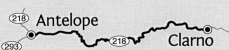

Clarno

- **Clarno Cemetery**
  (*0.8 miles north of Clarno*)
  The gravel road climbs more than 400 feet to this cemetery that dates to the 1880s.

- **Tillotson Cemetery** (*1.2 miles north of the Clarno Cemetery*)
  This small family plot had its first burial in the early 1900s.

Clarno rock formations

Clarno to Fossil

Distance:
   19.2 miles

Directions:
   From the Clarno Grange, go west on Highway 218 toward Fossil.

Points En Route

(mileage from the Grange Hall)

0.1 miles:
   Crossing John Day River.

0.2 miles:
   Clarno Recreation Site.

2.2 miles:
   OMSI Hancock Field Station.

2.7 miles:
   Fantastic rock formations.

3.0 miles:
   Picnic area, restrooms, hiking trails.

3.2 miles:
   Clarno Unit John Day Fossil Beds National Monument with picnic area, hiking trails, and restrooms. Geologist Thomas Condon discovered the John Day Fossil Beds in the 1860s. The formations known as the Palisades are 70 million-years old and span five geologic epochs. Three easy to moderate hiking trails, approximately a quarter-mile each, originate near the parking area where several signs describe the flora and geologic formations. The "Palisades Trailhead" is 0.3 miles west of the picnic area. The "Trail of the Fossils" affords magnificent views of the rock formations and fossils in the rocks. The "Clarno Arch Trail" leads to petrified logs and natural erosion cuts in the rocks. The "Geologic Time Trail" takes the hiker back 50 million years at a rate of 37,000 years per foot.

6.9 miles:
Weathered outbuildings.

9.6 miles:
   Pine Creek Recreation Area kiosk.

10.4 miles:
   Pine Creek Ranch with a dilapidated barn and corrals.

13.8 miles:
   Windy Ridge Ranch. The road begins a winding, descent from here.

16.3 miles:
   Picturesque, weathered barn with a double cupola.

19.1 miles:
   Fossil (IOOF) Cemetery; dates to the 1880s.

19.2 miles:
   Fossil

Fossil

Elevation: 2,677 feet

Location:
44.59.984 N • 120.12.817 W

Services:
gas, food, lodging, B&B, RV Park

Fossil, population 555, is the seat of Wheeler County, Oregon's smallest with a population of just over 1,500. The town was settled in 1869, opened its post office in 1876, and was incorporated in 1891. When Thomas Hoover, the town's first postmaster, discovered mastodon bones on his ranch, he suggested Fossil as the name for the community. Although

people digging at the fossil beds

fossil digging is prohibited in the nearby John Day Fossil Beds, it is permitted in Fossil in a designated area on the grounds of the local high school. Simply walk across the football field to the layers of rock that are full of fossil plants, trees, seeds, insects, and an occasional fish or salamander – 35 species have been identified thus far. If lucky, you may unearth a Metasequoia, the Oregon State Fossil. A walking-tour map of the community is available at most downtown businesses, and a Bluegrass Festival and Antique Car Cruise-In are held every July. Besides digging fossils, visitors can fish or raft the nearby John Day River, and rock hounds can collect thunder eggs, agates, opal, jasper and quartz crystal.

Points of Interest

- **Thomas Hoover House**
  (1st and Adams)
  Hoover came to the area in 1870 and built this house in 1882.

- **Fossil Beds**
  (Wheeler High School on B Street)
  During its construction in 1949,

Pine Creek School

the fossil beds were unearthed during the excavation of the football field. The school now charges a small fee to dig on its property. Digging equipment is available at the site, and workers offer advice and sometimes samples.

- **Fossil Elementary School** *(between 1st and Broadway on Washington)*
  In 1923 this became the third school at this site, replacing an 1887 structure that was built after a fire destroyed the first in 1882.

- **Baptist Church**
  (1st and Jay)
  The original building was constructed in 1881, with an addition made in 1903.

- **Masonic Lodge**
  (1st and Washington)
  Opened as a general store in 1881 and is the oldest store building in Fossil.

- **Pine Creek School**
  (1st and Washington)
  Built in 1889 and moved here recently, the schoolhouse now serves as an interpretive center during the summer. A 1930s sheepherder's wagon, completely outfitted, sits next to the school.

- **Fossil Bank** *(1st and Washington)*
  Built in 1920, this brick structure replaced a wooden building but contains the original vault.

82

Fossil

- **Arthur Glover City Park**
  (*1st Street*)
  Named for a resident killed in
  World War I.

- **Antique Car Museum**
  (*1st Street*)
  Many oldies now occupy the
  former blacksmith shop.

- **Fossil Mercantile**
  (*2nd and Main*)
  After the mercantile opened in
  1883, the upstairs was the site of
  many dances, parties and plays.

- **Chevrolet Car Dealership**
  (*2nd and Main*)
  Has been selling cars at this
  location since 1927.

- **Mortimer House**
  (*between 2nd and 3rd on Jay*)
  A unique structure formed by
  combining three homes. Allegedly,
  one of the three buildings was the
  town's "Red Light" house in the
  1920s.

- **Wheeler County Courthouse**
  (*between 3rd and 4th on Adams*)
  Built in 1901, this is one of
  only two remaining original
  courthouses in the state. The
  bricks used in its construction
  were made at a plant a half-mile
  from the city center.

- **Fossil Stage Stop**
  (*3rd and Washington*)
  In the 1880s this house was a stage
  stop and roadhouse. It was converted
  to a family dwelling in 1917.

- **Kelsay House** (*5th and Jefferson*)
  This 1884 house is home to a
  descendant of an early Fossil
  business owner.

- **Hendricks House**
  (*6th and Washington*)
  Erected in 1886, this house is
  still inhabited by a relative of the
  original owner.

- **Fossil United Methodist
  Church** (*7th and Main*)
  First services took place here on
  Christmas Day in 1877.

- **Masonic Cemetery** (*off D
  Street*)
  Dates to the 1880s.

- **Wilson Guest Ranch**
  (*2.2 miles northwest of Fossil at
  16555 Butte Creek Road*)
  Besides a bed and breakfast,
  this fifth generation, 9,000 acre
  working ranch has hiking trails,
  horseback rides, bird watching,
  and four wheeler tours of the
  history and geology of the area.

Wheeler County Courthouse

- **Kinzua** (*10.0 miles east of
  Fossil on Kinzua Road*)
  A sawmill and company town
  once nestled here on the Blue
  Mountains. Now a six-hole golf
  course lies on part of its grounds.

Fossil to Mayville

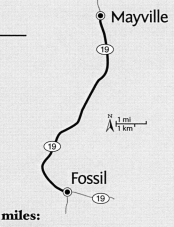

Distance:
7.0 miles

Directions:
At 7th and Washington in Fossil,
turn right onto Highway 19 and
travel north.

Points En Route

(*mileage from the corner of 7th and
Washington*)

0.8 miles:
Buttercreek Road. Nearby are
beautiful rock outcroppings and
abandoned houses.

4.3 miles:
Cummings Hill Summit;
Elevation 3,310 feet.

4.9 miles:
A solitary windmill in a hay field.

7.0 miles:
Mayville

Mayville

Elevation: 2,954 feet

Location:
45.04.941 N • 120.11.556 W

Services:
none

The community, once a stage stop between Fossil and Condon, was platted as 'Clyde' in the 1870s, but the name changed to Mayville when the post office opened in 1884. The name comes from the month in which the post office was approved. It also had a hotel, general store, and gristmill. Its two-room schoolhouse was built in 1894 but burned in 1989.

Mayville IOOF Hall

Points of Interest

- **I.O.O.F Hall** (*corner of Carter Hill Road and Highway 19*)
  The hall was constructed in 1895, replacing a building at the site that burned. The lower floor held a general store, and the upstairs served as a meeting place and dance hall an also housed the Ladies Aid Society.

- **Old Garage**
  (*Carter Hill Road and Quinn*)
  A brick structure where many cars were repaired in its day.

abandonded building
near Mayville

Mayville to Condon

Distance:
11.6 miles

Directions:
From the intersection of Carter Hill Road and Highway 19, continue south.

Points En Route

(*mileage from intersection of Carter Hill Road and Highway 19*)

0.8 miles:
Cemetery Road. The nearby Mayville Cemetery dates to 1886. One sad gravesite is that of Henry Beck, whose headstone reads, "Poorly born, poorly lived, poorly died and no one cried."

3.1 miles:
Dyer State Park. Picnic areas and primitive restrooms.

6.3 miles:
Crossing Thirtymile Creek Canyon. Old home below the bridge.

6.7 miles:
Thirtymile Cave (left of the highway). This large lava tube was used as a storage facility for wagon masters hauling freight from The Dalles.

8.8 miles:
Glimpses of the old wagon road over the next 2.5 miles.

11.5 miles:
Old homestead.

11.6 miles:
Condon

Condon

Condon Hotel

Elevation: 2,914 feet

Location:
45.14.110 N • 120.11.092 W

Services:
gas, food, lodging, RV Park

The first homesteader in Condon, the county seat of Gilliam County (pronounced GILL – um), was shepherd William Potter in 1883. The town was named for Harvey Condon, a local lawyer and nephew of famed naturalist and geologist Thomas Condon. The town was home to two Nobel Prize winners: Linus Pauling, who won in 1954 for Chemistry and again in 1962 for Peace; and William Murphy, who won in 1934 for Medicine. It is also the site of the only Powell's Book outlet outside the Portland Metropolitan area. In an attempt to boost its economy, Condon today is offering incentives to business people willing to locate here.

Points of Interest

- **Condon City Hall** (*128 Main*)
  Built in 1899.

- **Old Bank Building** (*135 Main*)
  Built in 1899.

- **Jackson Country Flower's and Powell's Book Store**
  (*201 Main*)
  The 1897 building, originally constructed as a confectionery, contains a soda fountain and counter, a variety store, a flower shop, and a book emporium.

- **Condon Hotel** (*202 Main*)
  This 1918 structure was built after fires destroyed the 1885 and 1890 buildings that preceded it. The hotel was totally remodeled in 2001 and is again open for business.

- **Liberty Theatre** (*212 Main*)
  Opened in 1892.

- **Barber and Bath House**
  (*217 Main*)
  When it opened in 1897, this was for use by men only.

- **Condon Library** (*310 Main*)
  Built in 1903.

- **Portwood-Hebert House**
  (*312 Gilliam*)
  Built in 1902 and still one of the grande dames of the community.

- **Mercer-Ashenfelter Cars**
  (*Main and Washington*)
  First opened its doors in 1918.

Rice Cabin

- **M and A Hardware Store**
  (*Main and Spring*)
  This was originally named Barker Brothers Store, Condon's first general store.

- **Flatts Automotive**
  (*Main and Walnut*)
  Opened in 1924 and now the home of Fatland Tires.

- **Linus Pauling Home** (*on Lincoln between Walnut and Fraser*)
  The boyhood home of the two-time Nobel Prize winner.

- **Victorian House**
  (*Walnut and Potter*)
  A picturesque home built in 1895.

- **Condon Catholic Church**
  (*Church Street*)
  The old church opened in 1925.

- **Condon's First Schoolhouse**
  (*Fraser and Church*)
  This one-room school, whose first teacher was Mollie Carter Portwood, has been converted to a private residence.

- **Condon City Park**
  (*John Day Highway and Wasco-Heppner Highway*)
  Condon has many natural springs, one of which helps fill the community swimming pool here.

- **Condon Historical Society Museum** (*Highway 19 next to the fairgrounds*)
  Buildings include the 1884 Rice Cabin, an 1890s tonsorial parlor, the 1905 train depot, the 1915 Brown Schoolhouse, the city jail, and an old caboose. Open Wednesday through Sunday from Memorial Day to Labor Day.

- **Burns County Park**
  (*adjacent to Historical Society Museum on Highway 19*)
  Picnic area, playground and restrooms.

Condon to Gwendolen

Distance:
7.8 miles

Directions:
From the Historical Society Museum, turn left onto Highway 19 and drive north.

Points En Route

(mileage from the Condon Historical Society Museum)

0.1 miles:
Four cemeteries – including Masonic, Knights of Pythias, I.O.O.F, and St. Joseph – are adjacent to each other.

7.8 miles:
Gwendolen

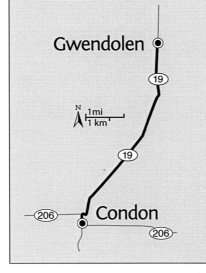

Gwendolen

Elevation: 2,506 feet

Location:
45.20.851 N • 120.08.444 W

Services:
none

Gwendolen was named for the daughter of the railroad tycoon whose crews punched the tracks through here in 1899. The post office opened in 1917 but was shortly lived. The school, also built in 1917, has been torn town. On a clear day from here you can see five major Cascade Peaks in Washington and Oregon.

Gwendolen grain elevator

Gwendolen to Clem

Distance:
7.5 miles

Directions:
From Gwendolen, continue North on Highway 19. Along this route, trees are scarce and wheat dominates the landscape.

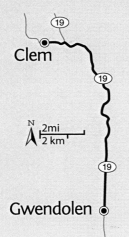

Points En Route

(mileage from the "Gwendolen" sign on Highway 19)

0.1 miles:
Site of Gwendolen School.

6.5 miles:
Turn left onto Clem Road.

6.6 miles:
Pavement ends, though a well-maintained stretch of road continues for the next 4.5 miles. You can avoid the gravel by taking Highway 19 to Olex and picking up the tour route at that point.

7.5 miles:
Clem

Clem

Elevation: 1,885 feet

Location:
45.25.250 N • 120.11.973 W

Services:
none

The once-bustling community of Clem is named for Clemens (Clem) Danneman, a German immigrant and Civil War veteran who began farming here in 1879, and whose house served as the stage stop. Starting with the 1905 arrival of the Union Pacific Railroad branch line, a community flourished. An attempt to form a new town, Welshons, on the other side of the tracks ended when the two communities united under the name of Clem, which once had a schoolhouse, grange hall, blacksmith shop, two livery stables, two saloons, and three stores – but no church, so services were held in one of the saloons. Today the area is the site of some grain elevators and a few, scattered homes.

Points of Interest

- **Danneman House**
  (across from schoolhouse lane)
  Home of the town's founder and the former Clem Hotel, the house is a private residence.

- **Clem School** *(visible from the Clem-Mikkalo Road)*
  This weathered, often-photographed 1884 school with a flagpole atop its bell tower closed in 1937.

Clem School

Mikkalo

Elevation: 1,470 feet

Location:
45.28.201 N • 120.13.986 W

Services:
none

Mikkalo was named after settler John Mikkalo, who arrived here in 1905 at the same time as the railroad. At one time, Mikkalo had a hotel, general store, blacksmith shop and several warehouses. In 1907 the school opened on the hill overlooking the grain elevators, and in 1908 the post office was established in the store, but closed in 1917. Today a few homes survive while the old store, now closed, stands empty.

old store front in Mikkalo

Clem to Mikkalo

Distance:
4.4 miles

Directions:
At the intersection of Clem Lane and Pennington Road, drive west and north on Clem Lane.

Points En Route

(mileage from the intersection of Clem Lane and Pennington Road)

3.6 miles:
Turn left onto Mikkalo Lane. Pavement ends.

4.4 miles:
Mikkalo

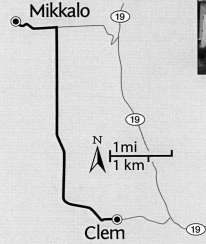

Mikkalo to Olex

Distance:
4.8 miles

Directions:
From Mikkalo, backtrack on Mikkalo Lane to French Charlie Road.

Points En Route

(mileage from the intersection of Mikkalo Lane and French Charlie Road)

0.8 miles:
Intersection with Clem Road. Continue east on Mikkalo Lane.

2.1 miles:
Intersection with Highway 19. Turn left and drive north.

3.1 miles:
Grain elevators.

4.7 miles:
New bridge.

4.7 miles:
Turn right onto Rock Creek Lane.

4.8 miles:
Olex

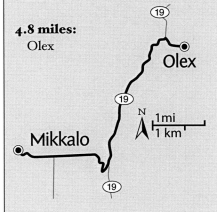

Olex

Elevation: 967 feet

Location:
45.29.993 N • 120.10.605 W

Services:
none

Opening in 1874, the Olex post office was the first in Gilliam County. The intention was to name the community "Alex" for local resident Alex Smith, but poor handwriting on the application led postal officials to read the name as "Olex," which remains the only such name for a community in the nation. In its heyday, Olex had two general stores, two blacksmith shops, a jail, hotel, saloon, church, drug store, meat market, and school.

Points of Interest

- **Olex Post Office**
  (*0.4 miles east on Rock Creek Road*)
  A marker here commemorates the site of the community's original post office.

- **Olex Elementary School**
  (*0.5 miles east on Rock Creek Road*)
  This 1880 school, the second in Olex, is now a private residence.

- **Olex Cemetery** (*1.1 miles past the school, east on Rock Creek Road*)
  Dates to the 1880s.

Olex to Arlington

Distance:
15.7 miles

Directions:
From Olex, return to Highway 19 and turn right toward Arlington.

Points En Route

(*mileage from the Intersection of Rock Creek Road and Highway 19*)

2.3 miles:
Old but well-maintained farmhouse.

3.8 miles:
Marion Weatherford Ranch. Weatherford Hall at Oregon State University is named after him.

4.0 miles:
Shutler Flat settled in 1861 by W.W. Weatherford, the first wheat farmer in Gilliam County. This was the first railroad station on the Condon Branch rail line as well as the site of the community of Shutler.

8.8 miles:
Weatherford Monument and site of the Oregon Trail.

12.7 miles:
Eightmile Road, part of the Oregon Trail. Site of George Washington Montague School, built directly on the trail.

15.3 miles:
China Creek Golf Course.

15.5 miles:
Columbia River RV Park.

15.7 miles:
Arlington

Arlington City Park—
Earl Snell Memorial Park

Arlington

Elevation: 307 feet

Location:
45.43.039 N • 120.12.186 W

Services:
gas, food, lodging, RV Park

In 1880, Elijah Ray was the first to settle in this area, then called Alkali, an important steamboat landing and once a Native American trading site. The post office opened in 1881 and the town site platted and the first school built in 1882. The name was changed to Arlington in 1885 and the town incorporated in 1887. Interestingly, Arlington was the county seat for five years, until an 1890 election turned that honor over to Condon. Old Arlington had several large warehouses, a general mercantile store, a bank, and other key commercial buildings. Most of the original community was flooded in 1968 when the John Day Dam – the state's leading producer of electricity – was built and Lake Umatilla created.

Union Pacific car in Arlington City Park

Points of Interest

- **Nazarene Church**
  (Cedar and Main)
  Constructed in 1921.

- **Arlington Cemetery**
  (top of the hill on Main)
  Dates to the early 1880s.

- **Arlington Methodist Church**
  (Hemlock, off of Main)
  An aged church with an old church bell and a contemporary addition.

- **Bungalow Home** *(1st Avenue)*
  Great views of the river below from this location.

- **Arlington City Park-Earl Snell Memorial Park**
  (near entrance to Interstate 84)
  Two parks, side by side, with a swimming area, restrooms, and picnic areas. An old Union Pacific Railroad car sits nearby.

- **Old Home** *(2nd and Hemlock)*
  One of the oldest houses in Arlington.

- **Sears Roebuck House**
  (3rd and Hemlock)
  Purchased from the catalog and ready to assemble.

- **Four-Mile Oregon Trail Interpretive Site** *(7.2 miles east of Arlington on Highway 19)*
  Hike a section of the original Oregon Trail. Wagon ruts are visible.

Oregon Trail ruts

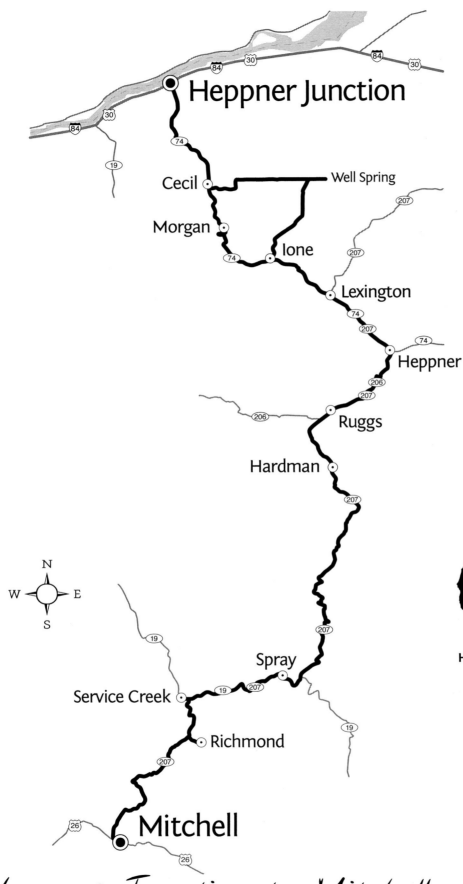

Heppner Junction

Cecil

Well Spring

Morgan

Ione

Lexington

Heppner

Ruggs

Hardman

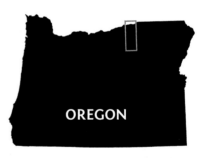

OREGON

Spray

Service Creek

Richmond

Mitchell

N
W   E
S

Heppner Junction to Mitchell

Following Flood-Ravaged Willow Creek

Heppner Junction to Mitchell (145 miles)

This journey along the Blue Mountain Scenic Byway begins on a beautiful roadway near the Columbia River, follows an old rail line along Willow Creek to Heppner, and eventually ends on the edge of the Blue Mountains, which were created more than 140 million years ago and cover more than 4,000 square miles of Oregon's north-central and northeastern regions.

Along the way the route crosses into three counties: Gilliam, Morrow, and Wheeler. Native Americans once used this route as a migration path between their salmon fishing grounds along the Columbia and their hunting grounds in the Blue Mountains. During the region's gold rush in the 1860s, it became important to miners traveling south to the gold fields. Today it is the main connection between Interstate 84 and Heppner, the Morrow County seat.

John Day River near Spray

Heppner Junction (exit 147 on I-84) to Cecil

Distance:
13.6 miles

Directions:
From exit 147 on Interstate 84, proceed south on Highway 74, the Blue Mountain Scenic Byway.

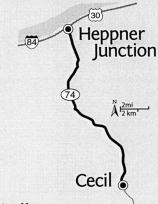

Points En Route

(mileage from the stop sign at the exit 147 off ramp)

0.1 miles:
Information Kiosk. The interpretive sign describes the Willow Creek Valley, Blue Mountains, and the Scenic Byway, and the impact that the creek and its floods have had on the people and the land.

3.6 miles:
Crossing Willow Creek.

6.9 miles:
Abandoned homestead.

8.1 miles:
Morrow County line.

13.6 miles:
Cecil

Cecil

Elevation: 634 feet

Location:
45.37.159 N • 119.57.433 W

Services:
none

Cecil began as an important watering stop on the Oregon Trail. In 1867 emigrant William Cecil had wagon trouble here, stopped to make repairs, and ended up staying. The community prospered as a rest area and stage stop with "The Well," located in the center of town near the old general store, serving as a public watering trough. The 1964 flood did serious damage to the rail line, eventually leading to is complete removal in 1994. When the tracks were pulled, the store closed and Cecil's commercial existence ended.

Points of Interest

- **Cecil General Store**
  (across the bridge on Willow Creek)
  The now-closed store opened in 1903 and is now full of antiques. It sits near the old railroad line and depot site. A sign on the store commemorates the 1843 Oregon Trail.

- **Cecil School**
  Built in 1902, but now a private residence.

- **Sheepherders Wagon** *(near entrance to town on Highway 74)*
  Worth a look and a photograph.

- **Krebs Ranch** *(center of town)*
  Established in 1916 and now one of the largest sheep ranches in the region.

Cecil General Store

Cecil to Ione

Option 1: Cecil to Ione via Morgan (see this page). This is the shortest route, along paved Highway 74.

Option 2: Cecil to Ione via Well Spring (see next page for option 2).

Cecil to Morgan

Distance:
5.1 miles

Directions:
From Cecil, continue south on Highway 74.

Points En Route

(mileage from junction of Highway 74 and Immigrant Road)

3.5 miles:
Old railroad bed on the right and basalt walls to the left are evidence of the power of Willow Creek.

4.4 miles:
Earthen Dam. Look for a concrete foundation near the base of the dam.

5.1 miles:
Morgan

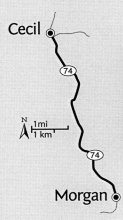

Morgan

Elevation: 787 feet

Location:
45.33.333 N • 119.55.269 W

Services:
none

The community started as the stage stop of Saddle, named after the Butte (east of town) that overlooks the community. Its first residents arrived in the 1870s, and the post office was established in 1882. For a time the community was called Douglas, after the postmaster, but when Alfred Morgan succeeded Douglas, the name was changed in 1906 to honor him. That same year the school opened; it closed in 1951. Until the 1964 flood, Morgan was an important railroad stop, though all that remains today are a grain silo, some abandoned houses, and a mobile home. The old depot sits on the side of a hill about a half-mile to the south.

Points of Interest

- **Morgan Cemetery**
  (0.5 miles east on Rietmann Road)
  Dates to the 1870s. Oregon Trail pioneers who died en route to The Dalles are said to be buried here.

Morgan train depot

Morgan to Ione

Distance:
8.0 miles

Directions:
From Morgan, continue south on Highway 74

Points En Route

(mileage from the Junction of Morgan Road East and Highway 74)

0.3 miles:
Concrete railroad trestle foundations.

0.5 miles:
The Morgan Railroad Depot on left.

1.6 miles:
Raised railroad bed, minus tracks, adjacent to the highway.

5.2 miles:
Grain elevator.

6.0 miles:
Abandoned home on Willow Creek. Watch for deer and coyote.

6.9 miles:
Neglected farm and basalt outcroppings.

8.0 miles:
Ione

Cecil to Ione

Option 2: Cecil to Ione via Well Spring (see this page). This is a longer route; 11 miles of it consists of well-maintained gravel that follows part of the Oregon Trail and leads to historical sites.

Option 1: Cecil to Ione via Morgan (see theprevious page for option 1).

Cecil to Ione via Well Spring

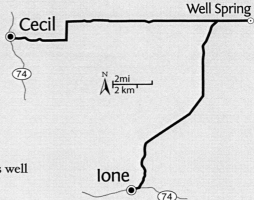

Distance:
24.3 miles (not including 5.1 mile backtrack to Morgan)

Directions:
From Cecil, continue south on Highway 74 and turn left on Immigrant Road.

Points En Route

(mileage from the junction of Highway 74 and Immigrant Road)

3.0 miles:
Intersection of Immigrant Lane and Morgan Road. Keep left, staying on Immigrant Lane.

5.4 miles:
View of Boardman in the distance.

7.0 miles:
Fork in the road, continue left on Immigrant Road.

8.1 miles:
Site of Ella. The former community had its own post office from 1882 until 1910 as well as a school, blacksmith shop, and small general store. The Butte above the site, called either Ella Butte or Well Spring Butte, was a key point for Oregon Trail emigrants. Today a single farmhouse stands at the site. Turn left on Immigrant Road, which is paved but rough.

9.3 miles:
The pavement ends at this farmstead. The gravel road is well maintained.

11.9 miles:
Intersection with Ione-Boardman Road. Stay on Immigrant Road.

12.7 miles:
Oregon Trail Historical Marker and Cemetery. Two pioneer gravesites are at this location. Colonel Joseph Gilliam, for whom Gilliam County is named, died near this site in 1848 as a result of a skirmish with local Native Americans.

13.5 miles:
Well Spring. Here are the remains of an important Oregon Trail watering hole that went dry in the 1960s. A dead locust tree, parched by the sun and contorted by the wind, leans onto the well's wooden slatted cover. Nearby, white fiberglass stakes mark the trail itself. Backtrack to the intersection of Immigrant Road and Ione-Boardman Road.

13.8 miles:
Old farm machinery in the field.

15.8 miles:
Intersection with Baker Lane. Stay on Ione-Boardman Road.

16.0 miles:
Pavement returns.

16.3 miles:
Intersection with Little Juniper Lane and Ione-Boardman Road. Continue straight. The one-room Lone Tree School, which opened in 1905, once stood at this intersection.

19.3 miles:
Abandoned farm and windmill.

21.9 miles:
Intersection with Ella Road; turn left onto Ella.

24.3 miles:
Ione

fields near Ione

Ione

Elevation: 1,050 feet

Location:
45.30.088 N • 119.49.556 W

Services:
food, B&B

The first resident of Ione was a sheepherder, who came to the area in 1872. The town was named for a little girl named Ione Arthur, who on a trip with her parents to see the Sperry family, ended up lending her pleasant sounding name to the community. Ione's post office opened in 1884, the first school was built in 1885, and the town incorporated in 1899. Ione is predominantly a farming community and a Highway 74 trade center for central Morrow County. Ione has a long and rich history and is making a major effort to return to its once prominent status in Morrow County. The school was severely damaged during the 1964 flooding and was rebuilt with unique, flood resistant construction. Many of the major downtown businesses north of Spring Street closed forever following the disastrous flood due to the loss of rail transportation.

Woolery House

Points of Interest

- **City Park** (*A and Main*)
  Restrooms, picnic area and playground. Featured are the 1906 fire hydrant and street signs from Ione's early days.

- **Train Depot** (*next to the park*)
  The 1900 depot has been converted into an amphitheater that hosts summer concerts and other attractions.

- **Historical Marker** (*in the park*)
  An information marker describes the importance of nearby Well Spring, an important stopping point for pioneers on the Oregon Trail.

- **Old Church** (*A and Main*)
  Serves as a preschool.

- **St. Williams Catholic Church** (*A and Main*)
  Built in 1948.

- **Ione Christian Church** (*D and Main*)
  This first church in Ione was constructed in 1911.

Train Depot

Ione

Points of Interest (continued)

- **Colliers Market** (*265 Main*)
  Built in 1920, Colliers was one of three grocery stores that existed in Ione's heyday.

- **Woolery House** (*2nd and B*)
  This former home of Joseph Woolery, an early Ione resident, land speculator, and mayor, is more than 100 years old. A memorial to him stands in the city park.

- **American Legion Hall** (*2nd and Greene*)
  Circa 1930.

- **Victorian Homes** (*2nd Street*)
  Several beautiful old houses line this street.

- **Car Dealership and Service Center** (*Spring and Main*)
  The old dealership with a service bay.

- **Willows Grange Hall #672** (*Willow and Main*)
  The grange hall sits across from the grain elevators.

- **Ione School** (*Spring Street*)
  Replaced the 1900 school, which stood at the corner of 3rd and Spring and was destroyed in the 1964 flood. The original bell is housed at the corner of the school grounds.

- **Old House** (*280 Spring Street*)
  This home with stained glass windows in the oldest home in Ione.

- **Highview Cemetery** (*north of town on the hill*)
  The cemetery dates to the 1880s.

- **2nd Street Victorians**
  Many beautiful, old homes line 2nd Street.

- **Valby Swedish Church** (*10.1 miles – 7.9 are paved – south of Ione Elementary School on the Ione-Gooseberry, to 60492 Valby Road, also called Swedish Church Road*)
  In 1886 Swedish descendants constructed this picturesque church.

Ione store fronts

Ione to Lexington

Distance:
8.2 miles

Directions:
From Ione, travel south on Highway 74 toward Heppner.

Points En Route

(mileage from the intersection of North Greene and Highway 74)

0.2 miles:
Ione Cemetery, dating to the 1880s.

0.5 miles:
Remains of a gas station and garage.

0.9 miles:
Old root cellar without a home.

1.1 miles:
Grain elevator, one of many in the area.

2.7 miles:
Jordan Grain Elevator, built in 1918.

6.1 miles:
Marshland and game preserve.

8.2 miles:
Lexington

Lexington

Elevation: 1,418 feet

Location:
45.26.721 N • 119.41.071 W

Services:
gas, food, airport

William Pentland, pioneer settler and land donator, named Lexington after his former home in Kentucky. An important shipping point, Lexington incorporated and opened a post office in 1885. In earlier times, Lexington competed with Heppner for the county seat, losing a close, tumultuous election. During that election, the town was set afire. Business owners held little insurance, but the Lexington faithful pooled financial resources to rebuild their town. Pictographs, graves and ancient artifacts from the Mayans have been found in the Lexington area.

Heppner Trading Post

Points of Interest

- **Wagons** (*A and East*)
  Several old wagons rest in the lot at this corner.

- **Lexington Baptist Church** (*B and Arcade*)
  Has operated continuously since 1895.

- **Victorian Home** (*B and East*)
  A large home and one of Lexington's oldest.

- **Heppner Trading Post** (*C and Main*)
  This building is actually the Lexington Trading Post. Look closely to see that the name Heppner was painted over the original sign.

- **City Park** (*E and Main, behind the Shell Station*)
  Picnic area.

- **Friendship Park** (*E and Main*)
  The Ladies Garden Society maintains this small picnic area adjacent to the Heppner Trading Post.

- **Lexington Cemetery** (*0.6 miles south on Cemetery Road*)
  Dates to the 1890s.

Lexington to Heppner

Distance:
  8.1 miles

Directions:
  Continue east on Highway 79 toward Heppner.

Points En Route

(mileage from C and Main)

2.1 miles:
  Farmhouse belonging to Doc Huber, an early Lexington doctor.

3.7 miles:
  Large old farmhouse.

6.7 miles:
  Kinzua wood products, no longer operational. A distant cousin to the lumber company that operated near Fossil.

7.6 miles:
  Willow Creek Country Club and the Morrow County Museum.

8.1 miles:
  Heppner

Heppner

Elevation: 1,930 feet

Location:
45.21.622 N • 119.33.319 W

Services:
gas, food, lodging

In 1873, the Heppner post office opened, the first school was constructed, and the town – named for Henry Heppner, owner and operator of the first mercantile store – opened for business. Cattle and sheep ranching and wheat farming are the main economies today. In June of 1903, heavy rains resulted in a flood that killed more than 250 residents (of a population of approximately 1,100) and destroyed much of the town. Many victims are buried in the local cemetery.

Morrow County Courthouse

Points of Interest

- **Morrow County Museum**
  (Main Street adjacent to the City Park)
  Pioneer artifacts, the early history of Heppner, and much information about the flood.

- **Morrow County Agricultural Collection of Farm Equipment**
  (Hinton and Riverside)
  Large display of farm machinery and implements.

- **Memorial to 1903 Flood Victims** *(Hinton and Highway 74)*
  Information and history of the tragic flood that caught Heppner by surprise. Of the main downtown businesses only the Palace Hotel, Roberts Building, and the Courthouse escaped damage.

- **City Park** *(Church and Main)*
  A small picnic area along with an old school that was moved to this location.

- **Memorial Park**
  (Willow Creek and Highway 74)
  Another park, dedicated to the many residents last lost their lives in the June 1903 flood.

- **United Methodist Church**
  (175 West Church)
  The church opened in 1876 and was heavily damaged by the floodwaters.

- **Morrow County Courthouse**
  (May and South Court)
  The bricks for the 1902 courthouse building were manufactured at nearby Balm Creek.

- **Victorian House** *(195 Court)*
  Beautiful craftsmanship and lots of gingerbread.

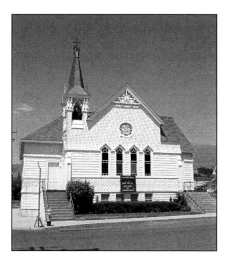

Heppner school   *United Methodist Church*

- **Morrow County Fairgrounds** (*off Fairview Way*) Home of the county fair since 1913.

- **Groshen's Spring** (*by the fairgrounds*) Perpetual fountain built by French immigrant stonemason Victor Groshen.

- **Heritage Museum and Library** (*Baltimore and Main*) An old brick building that contains many photos of the devastating flood.

- **Old Houses and School** (*end of South Main*) These structures were high enough to escape the flood. The old schoolhouse was built in 1875.

- **Masonic Cemetery** (*take Chase Street to Skyline*) Graves date to the 1880s.

- **IOOF Lodge** (*Willow and Main*) Constructed in 1901.

- **Masonic Lodge** (*Willow and Main*) Rebuilt in 1903 after the flood.

- **Fire Department** (*Willow and Gale*) Dates to 1899.

- **Bisbee Building** (*May and Main*) An old hardware store.

- **Hager Park** (*Hager and Corwin*) Small, neighborhood park. Limited facilities.

- **Willow Creek Dam and Reservoir** (*0.7 miles south and west on Highway 207 to Willow Creek Road, then left 1.0 miles*) 20,000 acres of water for recreation, electricity and flood control.

Heppner to Ruggs

Distance:
10.5 miles

Directions:
Follow Highway 206/207 south.

Points En Route

(mileage from the intersection of Main (Highway 207) and May)

0.3 miles:
A great view of the old school house, an old farm, and houses.

0.9 miles:
Road to Willow Creek Reservoir. Fishing, camping, picnicking, boating.

5.3 miles:
Vacated homestead.

10.5 miles:
Ruggs

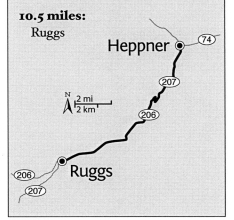

Ruggs

Elevation: 2,122 feet

Location:
45.15.824 N • 119.41.189 W

Services:
none

This community near Rhea Creek was established in the early 1900s, but now consists of a farmhouse on the creek, a park (whose main structures were burned in 2005), a picnic table, soda machine, pay phone, and an enormous grain elevator. At one time a general store and gas station sat nearby.

Points of Interest

- **Ruggs Park** Named to honor the area's first settler.

only house in Ruggs

Distance:
8.2 miles

Directions:
Continue southwest on Highway 207. You will encounter a climb of more than 1,400 feet and significant changes in the vegetation on the way to Hardman.

Points En Route

(mileage from the split of Highway 206 and 207)

0.5 miles:
Ruggs Ranch. A private hunting reserve.

7.8 miles:
An abandoned cabin with high fences to keep the deer at bay.

8.2 miles:
Hardman

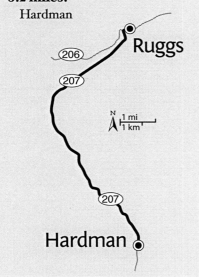

Hardman

Elevation: 3,567 feet

Location:
45.10.149 N • 119.40.952 W

Services:
none

Upon entering Hardman, travelers are greeted with the haunting sight of weathered, vacant structures and the eerie sounds of an occasional dog barking, windmills creaking, and doors flapping open and shut in the whistling wind. Once known as Dog Town, Hardman was formed by the merging of the two 1870s communities of Raw Dog and Yellow Dog, and soon became a major stop for stage coaches and freight wagons traveling north and south between the Columbia and John Day Rivers. The post office opened in 1878 and operated intermittently until permanently closing in 1968. Royce Hardman, one of two brothers who lived here in the 1870s, was a teacher who opened the first school in 1881. The community once boasted a large hotel, an IOOF Hall, jail, drugstore, flour mill, grocery store, and several sawmills, which were all torn down or vacated as modes of travel changed and Hardman's usefulness passed. Today some of the town is inhabited, but most of it is deserted.

Points of Interest

- **Hardman Community Center**
  This was originally the 1870 IOOF Hall. The source of water for the city, a well and hand pump was located near here.

- **Old Garage and Gas Station**
  (Water Street)
  Across from the Community Center.

- **Old Farm Implements**
  (Willow and 2nd)
  Neglected wagons, unused farm equipment, and old cars.

- **Hardman School**
  A marker points to the site of the 1881 school.

- **Hardman Cemetery**
  Take Rock Road 0.4 miles. The cemetery dates to the 1880s.

- **Hardman IOOF Cemetery** *(2.1 miles north and west on Rood Road, also known as Hardman Ridge Road)*
  Dates to the 1870s.

Hardman Community Center

Hardman to Spray

Distance:
34.2 miles

Directions:
Proceed south on Highway 207.

Points En Route

(mileage from intersection of Highway 207 and Rock Road/Willow Street)

1.6 miles:
Tree-lined canyon.

2.7 miles:
Deadman Hill Loop. (8-mile optional loop)

3.3 miles:
Rock Creek.

4.0 miles:
Unique rock outcropping.

5.7 miles:
Anson Wright Memorial Park. For day use and overnight camping, this Morrow County Park has restrooms, full RV hook-ups, tent sites, fishpond, and a playground.

6.0 miles:
Picturesque view of Rock Creek.

7.3 miles:
Chapin Creek. Wildlife viewing.

10.5 miles:
Deadman Hill Loop.

12.9 miles:
Morrow County OHV Park. Camping, picnic, primitive restrooms. Off-road vehicles welcome.

14.3 miles:
Boundary Umatilla National Forest.

15.8 miles:
Porter Creek, the boundary of Wheeler County.

17.4 miles:
Snow gauge.

18.0 miles:
Elevation 4612 feet.

19.2 miles:
Turn-off to Brill Prairie Recreation Area.

19.9 miles:
Fairview Campground with primitive facilities.

21.3 miles:
Crossing Kahler Creek.

23.1 miles:
Distant mountain views.

24.4 miles:
Tamarack Creek.

24.7 miles:
Boundary Umatilla National Forest.

26.3 miles:
Trees are sparse, terrain rugged.

26.6 miles:
Haystack Cemetery, a small, family burial site.

27.0 miles:
Haystack Creek.

30.0 miles:
Orchard.

31.6 miles:
Intersection of Highway 297 and Highway 19, turn right onto Highway 207.

34.2 miles:
Spray Riverfront Park. Swimming, boating, picnicking, restrooms, and fishing on the John Day River.

34.2 miles:
Spray

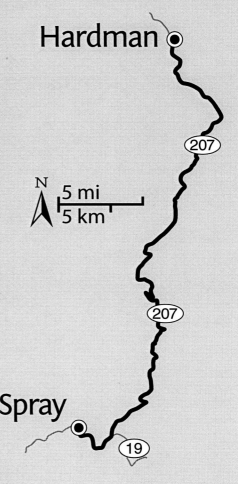

Spray

Elevation: 2,189 feet

Location:
44.49.888 N • 119.47.627 W

Services:
gas, food, camping, lodging

Spray was named after early resident and town founder John Spray, who moved here in 1900, the same year the post office opened. Spray offers many recreational activities, including fishing and rafting. The community flourished during the peak of the logging industry when several mills were in operation. The town of Spray incorporated in 1958 and today has a population of approximately 150 people.

Spray Pioneer Museum

Points of Interest

- **Spray City Hall** (*300 Park*)
  The center for local government.

- **Spray Pioneer Museum**
  (*402 Willow*)
  Housed in an 1890 church building. The old jail sits nearby.

- **Spray Schools** (*Park and Willow*)
  Built in 1920, this small school hosts many foreign exchange students.

- **Spray High School Dorms**
  (*704 Willow*)
  Not only for exchange students, but also for students willing to pay tuition for a small-school education.

- **Spray Rodeo Grounds**
  (*behind the school on Pine Street*)
  Small grounds that attract many participants and spectators.

- **Spray Grange** (*940 Pine*)
  Constructed in the 1920s.

- **Spray City Park**
  (*on the John Day River*)
  Day use only. Fish, raft and picnic.

- **Spray Cemetery**
  (*take Main to Waterman Flat, 0.7 miles from downtown*)
  Gravesites date to the early 1900s.

Spray High School

Spray to Service Creek

Distance:
12.3 miles

Directions:
From Spray, continue south on Highway 207.

Points En Route

(mileage from the south Spray city limits)

0.5 miles:
Scenic Vista of the John Day River and the start of the Blue and Strawberry Mountains, which cover 380 square miles. Native Americans called this area *Mah-Hah*, which means "much hunting and much food."

1.4 miles:
Kahler Creek enters the John Day River.

2.9 miles:
Crossing Snabel Creek.

5.5 miles:
Harper Creek.

5.7 miles:
Rock Creek.

6.1 miles:
Mathis Creek.

8.8 miles:
Juniper Creek.

9.7 miles:
Alder Creek.

10.0 miles:
Mule Shoe Recreation Area. Primitive toilets, fishing, picnicking, camping and boating.

10.9 miles:
River's Edge B&B.

11.6 miles:
Mule Shoe Creek.

12.1 miles:
Highway 207 South becomes Highway 19 North. Continue straight.

12.3 miles:
Service Creek

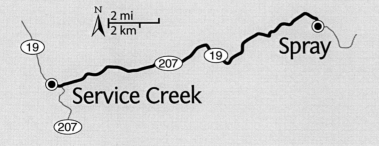

Service Creek

Elevation: 1,680

Location:
44.47.841 N • 120.00.468 W

Services:
food, B&B

This small community was named for the creek that borders it. The post office opened in 1918 and the community grew with the forestry industry. Today, Service Creek is mostly a stop for anglers, hunters, and campers.

Service Creek to Richmond

Distance:
6.4 miles

Directions:
From the Service Creek Store, return to the Junction of Highway 207 North and Highway 207 South.

Points En Route

(mileage from the Service Creek Store)

0.2 miles:
Turn right on Highway 207 south and head toward Mitchell.

0.5 miles:
Donnelly-Service Creek Park. Boat Launch, fish, and picnic with primitive restrooms.

0.6 miles:
John Day River crossing. From here the road climbs into the mountains, away from the river, and toward spectacular views.

4.7 miles:
Picturesque barn and pastures.

5.6 miles:
Turn left on Richmond Road, which is paved but rough.

6.4 miles:
Richmond (pavement continues 1.3 miles, past several abandoned farms and barns)

Richmond

Elevation: 3,208 feet

Location:
44.43.890 N • 119.59.522 W

Services:
none

Settled in the late 1880s, Richmond was once a town of 200 people. Apparently, a dispute arose during the naming of the community, with one of the residents allegedly acting like a Confederate in Richmond, Virginia; hence, the town's eventual name. A store was the first building constructed here, followed closely by a school, an IOOF Hall, a Methodist Church, a saloon, and a blacksmith shop. Fires and isolation from the highway have left Richmond as it is today, most deserted.

Points of Interest

- **Richmond Store**
  The first building in the community housed the post office.

- **Richmond Methodist Church**
  According to the resident family, the last services were held in the late 1960s. It is on private property.

- **Richmond School**
  Visible behind the old church.

Richmond Methodist Church

Richmond to Mitchell

Distance:
19.1 miles

Directions:
From Richmond, return to Highway 207 South.

Points En Route

(mileage from the Richmond Store)

0.8 miles:
Junction with Highway 207 South. Turn left and head toward Mitchell.

1.6 miles:
Richmond Cemetery Road. The cemetery, which dates to the late 1880s, lies approximately 0.4 miles east on a poorly-maintained dirt road.

3.2 miles:
Site of the former community of Waldron, which in 1879 had its own post office located on Shoofly Creek.

4.5 miles:
1909 Waldron School. Completely remodeled in 2004 at private expense, the remodel cost more than the original construction. A gorgeous setting for weddings, reunions, and socials.

5.6 miles:
Abandoned home and barn. Great views of the Ochoco Mountains for the next 13.0 miles.

18.9 miles:
Intersection with Highway 207 South and Highway 26. Turn left toward Dayville and John Day and Mitchell. The Mitchell IOOF Cemetery, dating to the 1880s, is located 0.3 miles to the right.

19.1 miles:
Mitchell

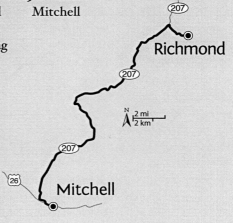

Waldron School

Mitchell

Elevation: 2,737 feet

Location:
44.34.018 N • 120.09.365 W

Services:
gas, food, lodging

Oregon Hotel

Because it was a prime camping spot with water and shade, Mitchell in 1867 became a stopping point on the mail route between Canyon City and The Dalles. In 1873 the post office and the first school opened; in 1893 the town incorporated and was named for U.S. Senator John Hipple Mitchell of Oregon. Located in a narrow, steep-walled canyon of Bridge Creek, Mitchell suffered from major floods in 1884, 1904, and 1964. The 1904 flood leveled twenty-eight buildings and killed two people. Several catastrophic fires have also swept through town, most notably in 1896 and 1899. These fires destroyed more than half of Mitchell, including many structures that had been rebuilt after flooding. Mitchell once had two stores, a blacksmith shop, and a hotel. In addition, thirteen lumber mills operated nearby, giving a rough-and-tumble image to the town that has since faded with the decline of the timber industry and the construction of the highway bypass. Today, Mitchell struggles to survive; most businesses are vacant, but you can stop and feed the resident goat at the gas station in the center of town.

Points of Interest

- **Oregon Hotel** (*100 East Main*)
  Across the street from the store. Houses a café.

- **Visitors Information Center** (*101 West Main*)
  Located inside the local laundromat, it comes with pay showers.

- **Mitchell Bank** (*103 West Main*)
  This was allegedly the last bank in the United States to be closed during the Depression. Built in 1918, it housed the post office until 1999 and now serves as a museum.

- **City Hall** (*108 Main*)
  Also serves as the community center.

- **Winebarger Hotel** (*112 West Main*)
  Built in 1880, it survived the floods and the fires.

- **City Park** (*East Main*)
  On the banks of Bridge Creek. Restrooms, picnic area and playground.

- **Brothel** (*210 Main*)
  Now a residence, the former "house of ill-repute" sits directly across from the Wheeler County Trading Company.

- **Little Pine Truck Stop** (*near the park*)
  Home to Henry, a black bear that was born and raised in captivity.

- **Wheeler County Trading Company** (*Nelson Street*)
  Built in 1890 on ground high enough to escape devastating floodwaters.

- **Mitchell School** (*High Street*)
  This building opened in 1901.

- **Old Houses** (*near the school*)
  Many of these homes, built away from the creek, are more than 100 years old.

Wheeler County Trading Company

- **Baptist Church** (*Hill Street*)
  Constructed in 1893.

- **Mitchell Cemetery**
  (*on Summit Prairie Road*)
  Granite gravestones date to the
  1880s.

- **Skyhook Motel** (*off Highway 26*)
  Brought in by trailer from the
  former community of Van-Port
  after the 1940s flood.

- **John Day Fossil Beds National
  Monument Painted Hills Unit**
  (*3.6 miles west on Highway 26*)
  One of the three parks that make
  up the John Day Fossil Beds
  National Monument.

former Mitchell gas station

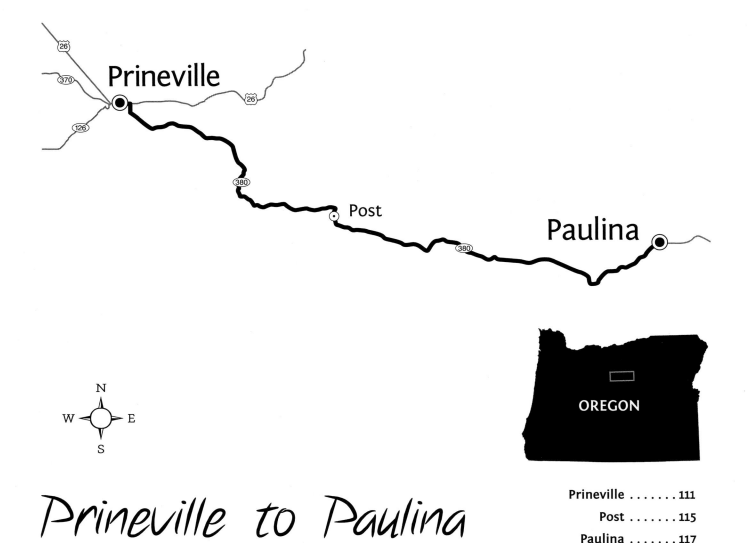

Prineville

Post

Paulina

N
W   E
S

OREGON

Prineville to Paulina

The Three P's in the Geographical Center of the State

Prineville to Paulina (58 miles)

This particular tour route is one of the shortest in any of the Roads Less Traveled books, but one of the most stunning and diverse. Juniper trees, unique rock formations, and abundant wildlife lie in wait around every corner. On warm days, unwary snakes bask on the pavement, and are frequently crushed by speeding vehicles. Travel in late spring can lead to encounters with large herds of migrating deer.

The route begins in Prineville, one of the Oregon cities hardest hit by the recession. The sojourn continues east toward Post, named for the postmaster and the job that he did, and then continues on to Paulina, named for the Paiute Chief of the Walpapi. This fifty-eight mile route has three stops, yet allows the traveler to explore some of the least traveled paved roads in North-Central Oregon. While in the mid-section of our state, make sure you stop for coffee, a snack, or gas at the old stores in Post and Paulina.

view of Prineville

Prineville

Elevation: 2,876 feet

Location:
44.18.188 N • 120.50.834 W

Services:
gas, food, lodging, RV, B&B

Prineville is the oldest community in Central Oregon and the seat of Crook County government. The town is named for Barney Prine, the first merchant in the newly formed community. Prine worked as a blacksmith in the back of his 1868 store, and served whiskey from a barrel in the front. Rumor says more business was conducted in the front part of the building than in the back! The Prineville post office opened in

Crook County Courthouse

1871 under the name of Prine, and was changed to Prineville in 1872. The town was founded in 1877 and incorporated in 1882. The local newspaper, *The Central Oregonian*, published its first newspaper in 1881. The railroad went around Prineville in 1911, a big loss for the burgeoning town. In order to survive, the town voted to build its own spur line to the closest track, nineteen miles away. The line ran timber from the Ochocos to local mills and was so prosperous, in fact, that no property taxes were levied here in the 1960s. A major fire in 1922 did considerable damage to the downtown core area. A current unemployment rate of nearly twenty percent makes Crook County the Oregon county most negatively impacted by the recession. Prineville, the only incorporated city in Crook County, lost more than $1,000,000 during between 2002 and 2004 and continues to flounder financially.

Points of Interest

- **Pine Theater** (*216 Main*)
  Opened in 1938.

- **Krider Estes Building**
  (*Main - next to the Pine Theater*)
  Built in 1879 as the Prineville Hotel.

- **Prineville Drug** (*221 Main*)
  The 1909 Drugstore is now Dad's Place restaurant.

- **Prineville Mercantile and Dry Goods** (*231 Main*)
  Circa 1910.

- **Bowman Museum** (*246 Main*)
  Formed in 1971, the museum is located in the 1909 Crook County Bank building.

- **First National Bank**
  (*3rd and Main*)
  This bank opened in 1907, replacing the wooden structure located at 5th. It now houses apartments.

- **Prineville Chamber of Commerce and Visitors Center** (*3rd and Fairview*)
  The Prineville Chamber of Commerce is the oldest in Central Oregon.

- **Crook County Courthouse**
  (*3rd and Dunham*)
  1909. The stone was quarried from local mines.

- **Ochoco Inn Site** (*320 Main*)
  Today the Lucky Penny Consignment Store, the inn was a vacation destination prior to the 1960 fire.

- **Prineville Hardware** (*395 Main*)
  Now the Book and Bean Bookstore and Coffee Shop.

- **Central Oregonian Newspaper** (*558 Main*)
Serving Prineville and the surrounding areas since 1881.

- **Crook County Fairgrounds** (*1280 S Main*)
Home of the annual rodeo, held every August.

- **John Luckey House** (*224 1st*)
Built in the early 1890s. Luckey was a Wasco County Deputy Sheriff.

- **Thomas LaFollette House** (*260 1st*)
LaFollette, a sheep rancher, built this home in the early 1900s.

- **George O'Neil House** (*304 1st*)
A rancher, O'Neil built his home in the mid 1890s.

- **Marion Reed Elliot House** (*305 N 1st*)
This 1900 home of an attorney was moved to this location in 1911.

- **George Cornett House** (*330 1st*)
Cornett was known as the "Stage Coach King of Central Oregon." He also owned several of the prominent downtown buildings.

- **George Cornett's First House** (*390 1st*)
Built in the 1890s.

- **Clifton and Cornett Store** (*1st*)
The first brick building in town opened as Hahn and Fried General Merchandise. It later served as a movie theater and is now law offices.

- **Ewen Johnson House** (*304 2nd*)
Circa 1894. Johnson was a successful rancher.

- **Eva Doak House** (*480 2nd*)
Built in the early 1880s, this home was constructed near the site of the first bridge over the Crooked River. Vigilantes hanged W.H. Harrison on the bridge in 1883. The river has changed course since the 1890s. A historic marker commemorates the site.

- **Ike Ketchum House** (*600 2nd*)
Ketchum, from Canada, opened up a shoe business in the early 1900s.

- **Hugh Larkin House** (*635 2nd*)
Built in 1912. Larkin opened the first hardware stores in Prineville, Bend, Lakeview, and Redmond.

Bowman Museum

Eva Doak House

Prineville

Points of Interest (continued)

- **Columbus Johnson House** *(640 2nd)*
  1906. Johnson was a cattle rancher who donated land for the Ochoco Viewpoint Wayside.

- **Jasper Wright Cabin** *(3rd and Elm)*
  Constructed in the 1880s, the old cabin was moved to this site and served as Prineville's first museum. Located in the city park.

- **Masonic Lodge #76** *(115 3rd)*
  The Masons organized in 1878 and built their lodge in 1923.

- **Cornett Building** *(231 3rd)*
  Fire destroyed the original building; this one was completed in 1923. Today it is the location of Prineville Men's Wear.

- **Williamson House** *(599 3rd)*
  Built in 1904 for sheep rancher John W. Williamson. The home became a boarding house after he was elected to the US Congress.

- **Masonic Lodge #76** *(5th and Beaver)*
  The Masons organized the lodge in 1878 and built this structure in 1920.

- **Elisha Barnes House** *(139 Beaver)*
  Built in the 1870s, this was the home of Prineville's first mayor.

- **Pioneer School** *(297 Holly)*
  Prineville's oldest remaining school; 1912.

- **City Railroad Depot** *(185 10th)*
  The city of Prineville has owned the railroad depot, trains, and track, since 1918. Look for the Mt. Emily Shay, the name of the 1923 locomotive that carried pine logs to the mills in Prineville, traversing a twelve-degree grade.

- **Juniper Haven Cemetery** *(0.6 miles north on Main)*
  Dates to the late 1880s.

Williamson House

Elisha Barnes House

Prineville to Post

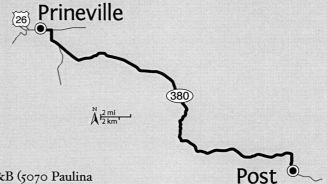

Prineville

Post

Distance:
24.8 miles

Directions:
From the intersection of 3rd (Highway 26) and Combs Flat Road (Highway 380 – the Paulina Highway), drive south toward Post on Combs Flat Road.

Points En Route

(mileage from the intersection of 3rd and Combs Flat Road)

0.2 miles:
Crook County High School sports complex.

1.3 miles:
Intersection with Juniper Canyon Road. Stay on Highway 380. The road will climb upward through rolling hillsides covered with stands of Juniper. Great views are found from this point all the way to Post.

3.2 miles:
Bella Vista B&B (5070 Paulina Highway).

4.7 miles:
Top of the plateau.

9.8 miles:
The abandoned home on the shoulder of the road is almost a "goner." A root cellar is located behind the home.

11.1 miles:
Old corrals and outbuildings with a good view of Pilot Butte in the distance (different that the one in Bend).

12.5 miles:
The road begins its descent.

14.5 miles:
A unique, red rock formation.

15.6 miles:
The road follows a dry creek bed.

16.5 miles:
Keep left, traveling toward Post. Prineville Reservoir can be accessed to the right.

17.0 miles:
Narrow valley irrigated by Beaver Creek. Look for the GR Cattle Company Ranch.

24.8 miles:
Post

abandoned home

red rock formation

114

Post

Elevation: 3,338 feet

Location:
44.09.429 N • 120.29.463 W

Services:
gas, food

Post is located at the geographical center of the state of Oregon. A post, on private property about 300 yards from the store, marks the exact location. The area around what is now Post was originally an 1855 Native American Reservation. The Reservation covered 10 million acres of ground, extending from the Cascades to the Blue Mountains. Government officials slowly took the land back and the last parcel,

Post General Store and Eatery

totalling 700,000 acres, was taken back for about two-cents an acre. Salmon used to run in the Crooked River as far as Paulina when Native Americans inhabited the area. The first settlers appeared in the 1860s after Camp Maury, a military outpost established in 1864 near the hills south of Post, opened to protect the emigrants. Major Steen, for whom Steens Mountain is named, commanded the fort. An unincorporated community located southeast of Prineville, Post was named for Walter Post, who served as the first postmaster in 1889 and was an 1885 landowner. The vast forests and several sawmills brought in more settlers; schools were constructed, roads improved, a Grange formed (1924), and then the depression came, starting the decline of the once prosperous community. Rock hounds, hunters, fishermen, hikers, and explorers find Post an oasis and take-off point for their ventures. The economy is mainly ranching and timber related. The Post store is home to the post office, gas pumps, groceries, a tavern and eatery.

Points of Interest

- **Post General Store and Eatery**
  The 1898 store, with its original wooden floors, offers a wide variety of merchandise – enough to take care of the needs of both locals and travelers. The post office, complete with mailboxes, exists inside the store. Old scales and bottles are displayed as well as trophy heads of elk, deer, and antelope.

- **Post Grange**
  The old building, located next to the store, has not been used in some time.

Post Grange

Post to Paulina

Distance:
29.7 miles

Directions:
From the Post Store, proceed east on Highway 380 toward Paulina.

Points En Route

(mileage from the Post Store)

Note: Be alert to snakes and ticks when exploring in the brush. The road frequently parallels the Crooked River. The irrigated alfalfa fields are a vibrant, spring green in mid-summer.

0.6 miles:
Abandoned house and barn.

1.2 miles:
Intersection with Newsome Creek Road. Stay straight on Highway 380. 0.5 miles to the right, on Newsome Creek Road, is the old "Shotgun School."

5.4 miles:
Antelope Reservoir access road. Stay on Highway 380. The Newsome Creek Community Church is not far from this intersection on the access road.

8.2 miles:
Drake Creek. Elkhorn Camp access road. Stay on Highway 380.

8.9 miles:
Private airstrip and hangar.

10.0 miles:
Teaters Road and a well-maintained, old farmhouse. Stay on Highway 380.

11.2 miles:
The Juniper Hills Preserve. Small, conical hills ribboned with color are found in the landscape.

13.8 miles:
LS Ranch.

13.9 miles:
Crossing South Fork of the Crooked River.

15.0 miles:
The valley floor widens. Adjacent hills have flat tops.

17.6 miles:
An old cemetery (Highway 380 at milepost 42).

18.6 miles:
The 1884 Glen Stage Stop. This log structure with an addition and several outbuildings are located at the intersection of Highway 380 and Camp Creek Road.

22.6 miles:
A large, modern ranch.

23.7 miles:
Weathered outbuildings.

28.8 miles:
Home of the Paulina Amateur Rodeo (68001 Highway 380).

29.7 miles:
Paulina

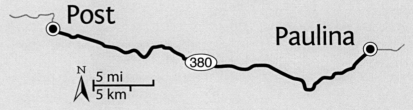

Juniper Hills Preserve

Glen Stage Stop

Paulina

Elevation: 3,690 feet

Location:
44.07.931 N • 119.58.034 W

Services:
gas, food

Paulina was named after Chief Paulina, leader of the Northern Paiute Indians. The small community was settled in 1870, and the post office opened in 1882 with John Faulkner as postmaster. The first general store opened in 1905, only to burn to the ground. In 1906, Fred Mosier built the first restaurant and saloon that burned in 1929. The first hotel opened in 1906 and the school in 1908. The current Paulina Store was constructed in 1917 and houses the post office and saloon. Located inside the store is the community's first water pump where locals came to get water from the community well. The Paulina Amateur Rodeo has been held annually on Labor Day since 1950.

Paulina General Store

Points of Interest

- **Paulina General Store and Post Office**
  Various food, hardware and personal items are stocked. An old cash register, old grocery items, and other antiques are displayed inside the store.

- **Paulina Grange**
  Moved to this site next to the store, the building also serves as the local dance hall and once was a clothing store.

- **Faulkner House**
  (one block from the store)
  Built in 1910.

- **Paulina Elementary School**
  Built in the 1960s to replace the 1908 building. The walls are painted with scenes from Paulina's past.

- **Paulina Community Chapel**
  Originally the Beaver Creek School, the building was moved to this location.

Paulina Community Chapel

Notes

About the Author

Author Steve Arndt grew up in rural Independence, Oregon during the state's centennial, a setting that kindled his curiosity about the region's history.

His uncle, William Gilbaugh, now a retired Washington State park ranger and noted northwest photographer, further ignited his passion by occasionally taking Steve on tours of Oregon and Washington back roads and byways.

After earning a degree in elementary education from Oregon College of Education (now Western Oregon University), Steve completed advanced degree coursework in special education at OCE, school administration at Portland State University, and his school superintendent credentials at the University of Oregon. In his 40-year career in education, Steve served various Oregon public schools as teacher and administrator, and completed his last nineteen years in higher education as senior associate professor of teacher education, including ten years as a department chair.

Steve, his wife Diane, and their now-grown children have spent many weekends and school vacations exploring Oregon back roads and off-the-beaten places. Today, their car is filled with child safety seats for young granddaughters that have begun road-trips with grandma and grandpa. Both Steve and Diane continue to fill important roles at the Woodburn United Methodist Church and enjoy volunteering in the Woodburn community and participating in various philanthropic groups and endeavors.

Although Diane, a retired music educator and professional singer, has no formal training in photography, she enjoys her role as photographer, organizer, and proofreader of Steve's book series.